The
Middlesex
Village Book

Margaret.
Happy Birthday
from Margaret, Ted
and family.

1989

THE VILLAGES OF BRITAIN SERIES

Other counties in this series include

Avon*
Bedfordshire*
Berkshire*
Buckinghamshire*
Cambridgeshire*
Dorset
Essex*
Gloucestershire*
Hampshire
Herefordshire*
Hertfordshire*
Kent
Lancashire*
Leicestershire*

Northamptonshire*
Nottinghamshire*
Oxfordshire
Shropshire*
Somerset*
Staffordshire*
Suffolk
Surrey
East Sussex
West Sussex
Warwickshire*
West Midlands*
Wiltshire
Worcestershire*

*Published in conjunction with County Federations of Women's Institutes

The Middlesex Village Book

Compiled by the Middlesex
Federation of Women's Institutes from notes
and illustrations sent by Institutes in the County

Published jointly by
Countryside Books, Newbury
and the MFWI, West Drayton

First Published 1989
© Middlesex Federation of Women's Institutes 1989

Countryside Books
3 Catherine Road
Newbury, Berkshire

ISBN 1 85306 039 9

Cover photograph of Isleworth
taken by John Bethell

The extract from John Betjeman's 'Middlesex' is taken from his
Collected Poems, published by John Murray (Publishers) Ltd.

Produced through MRM Associates, Reading
Typeset by Acorn Bookwork, Salisbury
Printed in England by J. W. Arrowsmith Ltd., Bristol

Foreword

The proximity of Middlesex to London makes the clear identification of the county rather difficult, but its people have a strong will and a desire to remain a County rather than simply a part of suburbia.

Faced with the official demise of our County, the Women's Institutes of Middlesex have fought hard to retain this identity.

One of the oldest counties in the land, Middlesex is steeped in history and, nowadays, with our modern development, it presents a fascinating combination which we are sure you will enjoy. We are proud of our heritage, and it has given us the greatest pleasure to compile this record of our progress – in the widest sense of the word!

Many thanks are due to all the enthusiastic members, and to their relatives and friends who have helped us, and sincere apologies to those whose contributions have had to be omitted through lack of space.

We love living in Middlesex: come and visit us, and you will see why.

Anne Mack
County Chairman

Acknowledgements

The Middlesex Federation of Women's Institutes would like to thank all those members, their families and friends, including many local historians, who have worked so hard to research and provide information for this book.

Our thanks are also due to the following:

Mrs Eileen Bowlt who kindly read the proofs.
Mrs Irene Brewer (illustration for Hillingdon)
Mr Dennis Brownlie (illustrations Harrow-on-the-Hill, Ickenham, Norwood Green, Ruislip and Uxbridge. Also The County map)
Mrs Pip Challenger (illustrations for Greenford, Isleworth and Harmondsworth)
Mrs Alma Downes (illustrations for Forty Hill and Maiden Bridge)
Mrs M. Evans (illustrations for Cowley, Harefield and West Drayton)
Miss P. Francis (illustration for Grange Park)
Mrs P. Gedye (illustration for West Drayton)
Mr W. G. Groom (illustration for Feltham)
Mrs F. M. K. Harris (Harrow-on-the-Hill entry)
Mr Geoffrey Hewlett (Wembley entry)
Mr Edward Keeping (Kenton entry and illustration)
Mr Allen D. Marsden (illustration for Shepperton)
Mrs M. Morgan (illustration for Pinner)
Mrs Lesley Price (illustration for Shepperton Lock)
Mrs K. Share (illustration for Stanwell)

Finally, a special thank you to Anne Mack who co-ordinated the project.

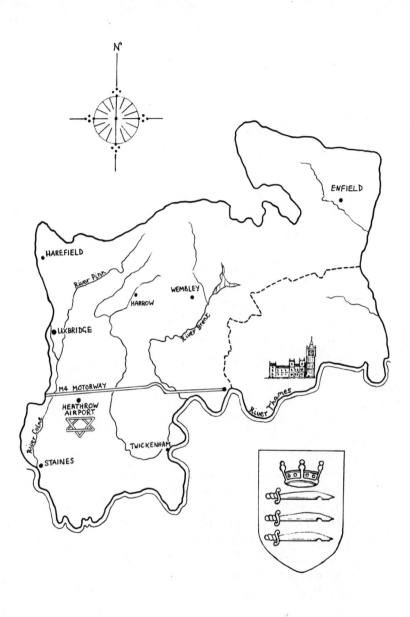

N

HAREFIELD

River Pinn

WEMBLEY

HARROW

River Brent

ENFIELD

UXBRIDGE

M4 MOTORWAY

HEATHROW
AIRPORT

River Colne

River Thames

TWICKENHAM

STAINES

County of MIDDLESEX

'Gaily into Ruislip Gardens
Runs the red electric train,
With a thousand Ta's and Pardon's
Daintily alights Elaine;
Hurries down the concrete station
With a frown of concentration,
Out into the outskirt's edges
Where a few surviving hedges
Keep alive our lost Elysium –
Rural Middlesex again.'

John Betjeman

Alperton 🌿

The name Alperton is derived from 'the farm of Aethelboert', and it was once farmland with apple orchards.

The oldest surviving record of Alperton was made in 1199. By the middle of the 14th century there were six small farms. In 1672 14 people had houses on which they were compelled to pay the hearth tax. In 1805 there were at least 21 houses, in 1831 the population was 199 and ten years later the census recorded 41 houses and a population of 242.

It was not until after the 1924 British Empire Exhibition at Wembley, which brought in many construction workers, that a considerable rise in population came about.

Among the early buildings in Alperton were two inns, the Chequers – licensed from 1751 and rebuilt in 1901, and the Plough. At the turn of the century the licensee of the Chequers (then known as the Horn) was an immense man weighing 35 to 37 stone. His name was Mr Ecclestone, after whom Ecclestone Place in Wembley was named. In 1851 there was also a beer shop at Vicar's Bridge and another, the Pleasure Boat, which took most of its custom from trippers on the canal.

Ealing Road, so called since 1914, used to be called Alperton High Street and before that Watery Lane.

There is still considerable drainage from One Tree Hill, so called because it originally only had one tree, the stump of which can still be found.

The main activity in Alperton used to be brick and tile making. The census of 1871 noted brickmakers, builders, hay dealers, labourers, gardeners, a carpenter, blacksmith and wheelwright in the village.

Alperton's most dominant personality was Henry Haynes (1831–1910). From a bellows blower in a blacksmith's shop in Alperton he rose to become a boatbuilder, wheelwright, wharfinger, supplier of building materials, coal and coke. In addition he built cottages, including Haynes Cottages in Ealing Road (where his name is preserved in Haynes Road, to the rear of the Keeler Motor Group premises), shops and a chapel. He also opened a brickyard and a sawmill and built a new hotel, of which he became licensee. At one time he owned about 70 of the 100 buildings in Alperton village, and employed nearly the entire labourforce of 150 people.

Henry Haynes had 21 children by his Irish wife, Harriet Martin (1836–1906). Many of these died in infancy and it was his second son, born about 1865, who succeeded to his business. In 1866 the Haynes family moved from the Pleasure Boat into the new Alperton Park Hotel, which thereafter remained their permanent residence. Although a jack-of-all-trades, Haynes was principally a builder.

Alperton Hall stood on the north side of Stanley Avenue, and was bought by Haynes in 1885. It was later used as a private school and then as the Imperial Yeomanry School. A memorial plaque on the wall south east of the altar in St James' church (in Stanley Avenue and soon to be rebuilt) recalled the army officers garrisoned nearby. This very first school in the area was for their daughters. Incorporated into Wembley Grammar School and now part of Alperton High School, part of the old house was demolished, but the entrance still exists.

The first Board Schools in the district opened in 1878 and, though somewhat renovated, still stand in Ealing Road. The log books show the School Governor's weekly signature when checking the attendance. He was William Perkin, knighted in 1906, a chemist who in his workshop near the Ealing Road end of Mount Pleasant, discovered mauve, which led to the foundation of the aniline dye industry. Not finding anyone in England who was interested, he took his formula to Germany. Subsequently ICI had to buy it back for this country! A framed piece of cloth dyed with the original mauve dye hangs on a college wall at Leeds University.

Alperton in the 1930s was still quite a village on its own. In the morning one could walk Ealing Road at 7 am and see the hand-pushed milk trolleys of Alperton Park, Leen's, Davies and Dowling Dairies, starting on their daily rounds. At Mount Pleasant one could meet the horses and carts of Chambers (contractors) going off to work. The Grand Union Canal also came to life early in the day. It was well used then by the horse-drawn refuse barges conveying refuse from Paddington for disposal. There were timber barges feeding Atcraft furniture factory and coal barges feeding the Key Glass Works. These were two of the larger employers, Glacier Metal being the largest (300 employees). One of the last blacksmith/farriers in the district had a shop in Manor Farm Road, where Ware's the builder's merchants have their sand pit.

There was also a little farming still done. Cleary's farmhouse 'Killarny' stood next to the Pleasure Boat, with farm buildings at the rear. They farmed grassland where Bilton Road area is now. Kennedys, who lived in Ealing Road with buildings at the rear, farmed pigs. There were eight terraced cottages between Kennedys and Alperton station. These have been demolished, but the footings can be seen through the grass verge at the front of Alperton school. Two cottages with large gardens stood between the station and Bridgewater Road. These were demolished and Alperton Bus Garage developed in 1934. The Wembley sewage farm was sited in Alperton Lane where the Council works are now.

The North Circular Road, from Seven Arches to Hanger Lane, had not then been completed, and all traffic going south had to go through Wembley and Ealing Road, making this a busy thoroughfare. The Abbey estate, not then developed, was an area of brambles and bushes, where rabbits

11

could be found. A horse watering trough used to stand outside The Plough public house.

Times have changed since the large employers have gone, and now there are small businesses flourishing in the area. Change has indeed come to the village of Alperton over the centuries.

Ashford 🌿

One John Ketch was 'had-up' in 1662 for breaking down the church doors and using 'opprobrious words against the government'. In the 1980s, things were still happening when an armed robbery at a small local bank made the national news. All this, where once the river Ash was forded, in the hamlet of Exeford ... Echelford ... Assheford; now a sizeable residential community, with pleasant parks. The Ash, unseen by motorists, runs today through the leafy roundabout which replaced a bridge built in 1789, at the end of the Staines by-pass.

Held in the Hundred of Spelthorne by the Abbot of Westminster, Ashford was annexed at the Dissolution of the Monasteries to Hampton Court. Henry VIII then leased it to Richard Ellis of his household, the lease changing hands over the centuries.

St Matthew's church, the third on the site, built in 1858 of Kentish ragstone, has a 16th century brass surviving from the earlier building.

A grassy roundabout near the church is a token indication of the long-gone village green, on which once stood the venerable 'town tree'. Nearby is the old King's Head pub and the horse trough.

At the opposite end of Ashford, behind iron gates incorporating red dragons, stands St David's School for Girls, of which the Queen is patron. Founded in 1716, in London, it was then a charity school for boys of Welsh parents. A hint of equality was introduced later with the admission of six girls and female supremacy triumphed in 1882, when it was named The Welsh Girls School. The present mock-Gothic building was opened in 1857 by Prince Albert, who alighted at the purpose-built station (previously a halt) from Waterloo. Princess Margaret visited the school for its centenary.

A rather different establishment arrived in 1870. The West London School, famed locally for its brass band, was founded to give orphaned and neglected children a fresh start in the country. The sad end to the lives of 55 of these hopefuls is recorded on the angel-topped war memorial. The school was later adapted as a remand centre.

The main thoroughfare, Church Road, still retains a 'village' feel, with small shops. The draper's, opposite the old fire station, is a nostalgic delight with its pre-war fittings. The Durhams came here in 1946 and will sell anything, from a single handkerchief to knee-length knickers! The need for 'a nice bit of haddock' is met by G. Powlson & Sons, poulterers and fishmongers since 1947. 'Muggeridges', as they are known, can provide a good bed, mattress or chair as they have done since 1917.

Ashford Shoe Repairs has been living on near the station since 1913. On the wall is a grimy copy of the Factories Act for 1908–1944. The present incumbent has among his customers an Australian businessman who stops off in Ashford, leaves his shoes for repair, flies on to America and collects his footwear on the way back!

Industry has not noticeably impinged on Ashford. The orchards and fields that were here have been covered by houses rather than factories. People commute to Waterloo, work at Heathrow airport or drive to the larger neighbouring towns to work. The local gravel pits are mostly worked out and have been in-filled, or conserved as willow-edged lakes, beloved of anglers, bird watchers and water skiers.

13

Yachtsmen enjoy the Queen Mary Reservoir and the river Thames is an energetic walk away.

In 1975, Princess Margaret visited Ashford again, to open the community centre, and Mrs Odette Hallowes, the war-time heroine, opened its extension three years later. Charlie Adamson inaugurated the open-air pool opposite (now gone, alas) in 1936, by plunging in, aged 80. Charlie, it's said, invented the 'tick-tack' system used by racecourse bookies.

Pevsner dustily dismissed Ashford as 'one of the least rewarding Middlesex villages' and certainly, progress has obliterated nearly all buildings of interest.

The Clock House was of mellow brick and had the only public timepiece in the village; today, just the clock survives, in the recreation ground. Chattern House, where Ethel M. Dell, the romantic novelist came in 1907 and wrote her successful *The Way of An Eagle*, has gone too and only road names echo her stay here.

Near the church is a house that was rescued when Heath-row airport was developed. Stored in a barn for years, 'Greenoaks' was rebuilt in Exeford Avenue, brick by brick, after the Second World War. Its original site is now occupied by Heathrow's control tower.

Botany Bay

Botany Bay is a small hamlet in the north of Enfield, near its border with Hertfordshire. It grew as a settlement after the enclosure of Enfield Chase in 1777 and was shown as a village on Greenwood's map of Middlesex in1829. Its name seems to have been derived from its remoteness from Enfield, no doubt arising from local jokes about it being as far away as Botany Bay in Australia! Botany Bay has no church, no petrol station and the village school has been closed, but it has a fine hostelry and a strong cricket club and Botany Bay Women's Institute.

The WI home is a timber building, which was built and paid for by the members. During the Second World War it was requisitioned for a time by the army and, later, to house a bombed-out family. The 'Hut' is built in the grounds of East Lodge, one of the four lodges of Enfield Chase, where Tudor and Stuart kings and queens once hunted deer, now part of London's Green Belt.

Charlton ✺

Charlton was mentioned in the Domesday Book of 1086, when the manor of Cerdentone was recorded as having been held by Roger de Rames. Later the manor was given to the Prior of Merton and it passed into the hands of the Crown after the Dissolution of the Monasteries in 1538.

Until the early part of this century the parish consisted almost entirely of farmland and hunting ground. An old manor house, known as Charlton Court, had a mulberry tree in its kitchen garden, under which was a tablet to commemorate the longest foxhunt on record. King Charles II had hunted the animal all the way from Windsor Forest until it took refuge in the tree.

In the 1930s Charlton was a quiet, picturesque little village, with three farms, a few cottages and a whitewashed, thatched inn called The Harrow. The inn is still there, attractive with its thatched roof and low timbered bar, claiming to be the oldest pub in Middlesex.

Nestling alongside Charlton was the ancient manor of Astlam ('East Laleham'), which was covered by 8,000 million gallons of water when the Queen Mary Reservoir was opened in 1925. The third largest artificial reservoir in the world, it dominates Charlton and the M3 motorway runs along its boundary. However, it is still possible to sense the rural atmosphere that the village once enjoyed. The residents of Astlam were rehoused at the foot of the banks of the new reservoir. It is said that in times of drought the tip of the church spire can still be seen below the waters.

Both Astlam and Charlton were part of the vast Hounslow Heath and it is said that King Henry VIII hunted many times on Astlam common. The famous Wood family of Littleton Park (where the Shepperton film studios stand today) were lords of the manor, and the ancient cottage used by the gamekeeper can still be seen behind the housing estate at Littleton.

Cowley 🌿

Cowley's old winding main road has been forced into a straight line and is used partly as a by-pass for Yiewsley. Traffic is unfortunately heavy and fast.

The Canal at Cowley

The church of St Laurence is a little way out of the village. Mentioned in the Domesday Book and possibly founded nearly 1,000 years ago, this 12th century building is of flint supported by brick buttresses. The wooden turret and spire were built in 1780, the roof is supported by trestles on solid oak beams (tree trunks fashioned to shape) whilst at the west end there is a double gallery. The church has been very carefully restored from time to time and in 1951 was entirely re-roofed and the rafters, many of which were branches of trees, replaced by modern timbers.

There is a memorial on the church to the Reverend William Dodd who was hanged for forgery at Tyburn in 1777. Dodd was an author and had been at one time chaplain to George III. His brother was rector of Cowley and it is believed that he brought William's body from the scaffold to be buried here.

There are several 17th century cottages, including Barnacre and Old Vine Cottage, as well as Maygoods Farm and Manor Farm and of course the meeting point, The Crown Inn.

Three small rivers and the canal flow through Cowley. The Grand Union Canal came through in 1798 and for a time a daily service of horse-drawn packet boats connected with Paddington, hence the nearby public house called the Paddington Packet Boat, and trips are still run on the canal today. Further along to the north is Cowley Lock, now part of a conservation area, and on the side there is another old public house called The Shovel, now modernised into a steakhouse.

There used to be a branch of the Great Western Railway running through Cowley from Uxbridge to Paddington which closed in 1964 under Dr Beeching's 'axe'. There are now houses where the station used to be.

There are several small businesses in the village and a large building contractor's has planted its roots in Cowley. A State infants school, a Church of England junior school and two children's homes are also in the area.

Possibly the most well known place on the border of Cowley and Uxbridge is Brunel University which has a large conference centre, halls of residence, science centre and sports complex. Parties of foreign students during the summer months add an international flavour to the district. This large university is built on land that used to be occupied by the largest market garden in the South of England.

A paradise for fishermen is Little Britain lake, a very picturesque spot which brings much pleasure to lots of people.

Cranford

Cranford, on both sides of the 'Road to Bath', is so named from the ford where the bridge now stands over the river Crane, and is not the original of Mrs Gaskell's story of that name.

It is a small village, which ceased to exist as a separate parish in 1934 and is now almost a suburb of Heathrow airport, of which its inhabitants are only too aware by the constant stream of aircraft overhead, though no doubt a great many of them earn their livelihood there and in the supporting services. On the way to the airport from the east one cannot fail to notice Cranford – the Berkeley Arms and the Parade, with its unique chateau-type buildings with their little slated turrets. Many acres of this small village are in Cranford Park.

The village was mentioned in the Domesday Book and in 1200 the manor house was owned by William of Cranford. From 1618 to 1932 it was the home of the Earls of Berkeley and their descendants. The 5th Earl boasted that he could drive from his London town house to Cranford in his horse drawn carriage in one hour. Today on the busy A4 and the M4 it can take just as long!

In 1933 the estate was sold and is leased, on a 999 year lease, to Hayes and Harlington Council as an open space. Its woodland walks and playing fields have so far resisted the developers. The manor house has been demolished, the moat walls all that remain on the site. The river Crane winds its way through Cranford Park, with an ornamental bridge of fine stonework to cross to reach St Dunstan's church, with another bridge across the Bath Road.

The park has seen a great deal of history. Cockfighting used to take place in the woods and legend has it that in Quintain Field jousting tournaments were held. The site of Springfield was once used as an observatory. The Cedars House was designed by Isambard Kingdom Brunel, who lived there. The Red House, another interesting building, was owned by Thomas Morton Berkeley, 6th Earl of Berkeley, who when he died was carried in his coffin across the park to St Dunstan's.

St Dunstan's church in the park commenced its register of marriages and baptisms in 1564. The chancel and tower are portions of the original church built in the 15th century. The nave was destroyed by fire in 1710. The church has many memorials to the Berkeley family including the tombs of Lady Elizabeth Berkeley (died 1635) and Sir Roger Aston (died 1612), who during his lifetime was Gentleman of the Bedchamber and Keeper of the King's Wardrobe to James I. The Berkeley vault was one of four opened in 1936 when the floor of the church needed strengthening and the bodies were reburied in the churchyard. The coronet of the 5th Earl (died 1810), found in the vault, was made into the sanctuary lamp in 1937. The oldest of the peal of bells was cast at Aldgate in 1338.

The Berkeley Arms was an 18th century coaching inn to the west of the village. Here the hunt used to meet. Grantly

Berkeley, Master of the Hounds, was distinguished by his tawny-orange coat. One chase ended on the steps of the British Museum. The old inn was demolished in 1932 to make way for the Bath Road widening and was rebuilt as a motel.

The main London to Bath road was built through the village alongside Cranford Park. In 1750 the first mail coach passed through the village and also the Royal Mail coach from Hounslow. Alongside the Bath Road stood the Green Bank forge. The building, over 200 years old, still stands though the brickwork has now been covered with cement.

Many of the buildings on the Bath Road and High Street have been replaced by flats and offices, but a small, round brick building still stands in the High Street. This was the village lock-up, used to house offenders prior to their appearance before the magistrate, and is said to be one of only two surviving in the Metropolitan Police District.

Cranford has a primary school and a branch library and a modern community school which caters for all branches of education and recreation, children and adults.

East Bedfont 🌿

Bedfont, called 'Bedefunte' in the Domesday Book, has a long history. Situated on the high road between Hounslow and Staines, its inhabitants lived for centuries on the edge of lawless Hounslow Heath. Travel was a dangerous business, as was shown by an incident reported in the local newspaper in 1751. A gentleman riding near Bedfont was stopped by two highwaymen, who demanded money from him. When he tried to resist they attacked him with swords and pistols, leaving him to die of his wounds. A farm labourer found the poor man the next morning, lying where he had fallen.

This isolation was one of the reasons behind Bedfont's

most famous industry – gunpowder. The wild and remote Heath was ideal for the manufacture of such a dangerous product, local rivers and streams providing the power for the mills. Not everybody welcomed the new industry however, for in 1609 Sir Michael Stanhope, the lord of the manor of Bedfont, appealed to the king to stop the development of gunpowder mills in his area. James I was not unnaturally more concerned with the availability of this valuable product and did not respond to Sir Michael's request. He even excused the mill owners from their annual rent in 1619.

The gunpowder mills continued in use until the 20th century and expanded their operations considerably in the early 1800s. After the end of the First World War the industry declined and ICI took over the mills, closing them down in the 1920s. Some of the buildings still survive, but most of the site has been redeveloped for industrial use and housing.

Bedfont has two other claims to fame – sauce and peacocks! A famous sauce is said to have been concocted by Peter Harvey, landlord of the old Black Dog Inn, in the 18th century. Harvey's Sauce became extremely popular amongst the gentlemen of the time and the Black Dog became a regular haunt of the driving clubs of the Regency Bucks of the early 19th century. Commercial production of the sauce continued into the 20th century.

The peacock legend concerns two yew trees in the chur-chyard, which were said to have been trimmed into the shape of peacocks in the early 18th century. Thomas Hood wrote a poem about the Bedfont peacocks in 1822, claiming that they were two overbearing women of the village who had been punished for their haughty ways by being forever frozen into the shape of the birds. Another story said that they were the work of a rejected suitor of one of the women, who cut the trees into a public statement of his feelings about them being 'proud as peacocks'. However, yet another legend says that they were not peacocks at all, but fighting cocks, the local parson having a partiality for such birds!

Eastcote ✣

Until the 1920s Eastcote was just a hamlet in the area of Middlesex between Ruislip and Pinner. Four inns, a smithy, a few shops, a Methodist church dated 1847 and some villas of the same vintage, three larger and more ancient houses and several scattered farms filled what is now a parish of over 20,000 people. It was changed by the coming of the Metropolitan Railway, which made travelling quick and easy for commuters working in London. Yet the old village of Eastcote still exists within the present day suburb.

The Old Barn House in High Road is one of the oldest buildings still remaining in the old village. It dates from medieval times, and in its time has been a dwelling house, post office, workshop and a centre for village social activities. At the beginning of this century the day trippers from London would take tea in its extensive gardens, on their outings by horse-drawn trap, bicycle or by train.

Opposite was the village smithy which survived until the mid 1950s, marked today by a modern bungalow named 'The Old Forge' which has the original anvil in the garden. The Tapping family kept the smithy from the 1880s and their work as blacksmiths, wheelwrights and carriage builders was all part of village life.

The Black Horse was well known from the 18th century, being mentioned in parish records for vestry assemblies and annual sales of timber cut from Park Wood. Today it is a pleasant 19th century building with modern extensions, and the appearance of a friendly village pub.

'New Cottages' in High Road was constructed in 1879 as

one building, but is now three cottages. Their mock-Elizabethan design with white plaster and black beams, was the work of the well known Victorian architects Harold Ainsworth Peto and Sir Ernest George.

Flag Cottage dates back to the 16th century, but more recently was part of the Eastcote Place estate of Sir John and Lady Anderson, when it was known as Spring Cottage because it had its own spring water. It was rented by a Miss H. Carter in 1887 who ran a private school.

Eastcote House, dating back to c1500, was demolished in 1964, but the grounds remain just as beautiful though they have lost their focal point. The coach house, stables and the quarters for the outside staff, were ranged round a courtyard at the back of the house. In Elizabethan times one of the early Hawtrey's built a dovecote without permission. The present square dovecote which dates from the 18th or 19th century is probably on the same site and still features the revolving potence inside.

The walled garden, probably built in the 17th century, has been restored and in 1977 a Jubilee Project with the planting of herbs etc took place. A granite sundial was built in 1986 and in the same year a pergola, planted with laburnum and wisteria, was created alongside the dovecote. The walled garden is a perfect example of living conservation, with new features and imaginative plantings being added constantly.

Haydon Hall was built and owned by Lady Alice, Dowager Countess of Derby in 1630. Dr Adam Clarke occupied the Hall from 1824 until 1832, during which time he started the Methodist church in Eastcote. It was also demolished in the 1960s but the grounds are now a pleasant park and home to Eastcote Cricket Club.

Haydon Lodge, High Road, originally marking the main entrance to Haydon Hall, is one of the service houses built in the late 19th century, in mock Elizabethan style. Most interesting of all are the wooden supports to the porch, all carved to represent figures in different national costume. The lodge, which is raised on brick arches to protect it from flooding of the river Pinn, cost over £1,000 to build over a hundred years ago, and is a Grade II listed building.

Built in the 16th century, The Case Is Altered is believed to be Anna Slepe's cottage. It faced on to Giddy Street which later became Southill Lane. It was licensed to sell beer in 1828 and was largely re-built after a disastrous fire in 1890. In more recent times the Bedford family were well known landlords and have told of performances by the Eastcote mummers in the tap room at Christmas time. In the 1930s they had no spirit licence and beer was carried by hand from the cellars. Eastcote Cricket Club always lunched at The Case while the visiting team went to the Woodman in Joel Street.

Joel Street was one of the ancient lanes which led to the waste or rough pasture. The Woodman was originally built as a cottage about 350 years ago and did not become a beer house until the late 19th century. Mrs Fanny Pakes was licensee at The Woodman for over 50 years and was still serving customers at the age of 92 in 1933.

Highgrove House is the only one of the great houses of Eastcote still remaining. Highgrove stands on an ancient site occupied in the 13th century by the Hale family. In the mid 19th century Highgrove belonged to the Fuller family and later to the Warrenders, a wealthy Edinburgh family. The whole family of Warrenders were great benefactors to the local community right up to 1949. The present Highgrove was built in 1881, after a fire in 1879 left the old building gutted. Restored after another fire in 1978 it is now used by the borough council as temporary accommodation for home-less families. A small area of its once splendid gardens remains as a nature reserve cared for by local conservationists and schoolchildren.

Catlin's Lane may take its name from the Norman Abbey of

The Holy Trinity in Rouen, where relics of St Catherine were kept, and which once owned a small manor in the Ladygate Lane area of Ruislip as well as land at Pope's End, Eastcote. This probably accounts for the association with the lane and with St Catherine's Farm. The house is possibly 15th century with Victorian additions. It was occupied in 1851 by Edward Long and 1861 by Thomas Ewer, both members of well-known local families. Local residents remember St Catherine's Farm as the home of Councillor T. G. Cross, who did so much to serve the community and the arts.

Enfield ❧

'When I was a little girl I remember being taken for a Sunday School treat to Enfield. I also remember my mother telling me how, when she was little, she used to take her father's dinner across country to where he was working his land and tending his goats.' That part of Enfield is now covered with industrial buildings and Kingsmead School. It is hard to reconcile the Enfield of those days with the present. It is even harder to imagine that the village of Enfield was many years ago a triangle of grassland bordered by the seven acre Manor House estate, which is now a department store and pedestrian precinct, and the parish church of St Andrew, standing proudly as it does today just beyond the Market Square. In the middle of the Square is the village pump, restored as near as possible to its original site.

Enfield has many historical connections. Queen Elizabeth I spent part of her childhood at the Manor House and it was there that she and her brother Edward VI heard of their father's death. The building was finally demolished in 1929 having been at various times school, club and post office among other things. Legend has it that there was an underground tunnel leading from the house to St Andrew's church on the other side of the village green. The arrangements for the Gunpowder Plot were finalised by Guy Fawkes and his co-conspirator Garnett at Whitewebbs House, and although that building was destroyed another house of the same name was built nearby which is now a residential home. It is surrounded by a golf course now instead of Enfield Chase.

Just beyond the churchyard stands Enfield Grammar School, one of the oldest school buildings in the county and still used for the purpose for which it was originally built in the mid 16th century. A quiet leafy little backwater, Holly Walk, runs past the school and leads to a lovely row of old cottages and houses – Gentlemen's Row, which marked the western end of the village. A blue plaque on the wall of one of the houses indicates that Charles and Mary Lamb stayed there in 1827 when they lived in London. They liked it so much in the beginning, living in the country, that they took a house in nearby Chase Side, but they soon got tired of country life and moved to Edmonton which is three miles nearer to London, where they lived for the rest of their lives and are buried in All Saints churchyard.

The people of the village of Enfield were horticultural workers, each man working one or more strips of land around the village. Enfield still has a good reputation for horticulture, having many thriving garden centres and nurseries on its outskirts. In fact if you go to Crews Hill on a Saturday or Sunday you would do best to leave your car at home because the world and his wife seem to descend upon this area to buy their plants and equipment for what is now the nation's second most popular hobby – gardening!

The old village green is now a busy shopping centre with one main thoroughfare, called The Town, leading into Church Street. It has its share of banks and building society offices and the ubiquitous shoe shops but not so very long ago there were two thriving ironmonger's stores where one could buy anything from a clothes peg to a mangle or a galvanized bath. There was a piano shop and a steam bakery, several ladies hat shops and haberdashers and a teashop. One by one they have given way to supermarkets, DIY shops, 'fast food outlets', music shops and travel agencies indicating more than anything else the way life has changed even within fairly recent living memory. The only things that seem to have remained constant are the churches and the public houses!

Enfield is a lovely place to live, balanced as it is between London and the Green Belt. Its residents have the best of both worlds being barely a stone's throw from the city and almost in the country.

Feltham ﷽

There has been a settlement here since at least Anglo-Saxon times, since Feltham is mentioned in the Domesday Book. The name means 'the field village' and the surrounding area was still rural up to the 1950s and 1960s.

The 'old' church of St Dunstan was built in 1802 on the site of an earlier church. It is of brick, with a tower and a wooden spire. The 'new' church of St Catherine was built in 1880, by the station. Buried at Feltham is William Wynne Ryland, an engraver (the first to use the 'dotted style') who was hanged for forgery at Tyburn in 1783.

In 1634 the manor house and almost all the buildings in the village were destroyed by fire. The manor house was owned by Lord Cottington, Chancellor of the Exchequer and was rebuilt after the disaster.

The King's (or Cardinal's) river flows through Feltham. It was constructed in the reign of Charles I to supply the ornamental gardens at Hampton Court and rises from the Colne at Harmondsworth.

27

Blaize Farm once stood near the old church and was known as 'Nell Gwynne's Farm'. The story was that it was a trysting place for Charles II and his love, but there is another story that it was used by Nell's sister's husband, a highwayman by trade!

In the 1930s Feltham was just a straggling street, with a green and a village pond. Yet after the Second World War Feltham suffered greatly from unplanned industrial expansion and gravel extraction. It had a reputation as a market gardening centre, but much was destroyed by the gravel pits. Then in the early 1960s Feltham was transformed by the erection of a modern shopping centre and tall flats. One side of the old High Street was demolished to make way for the dual carriageway and a view which had changed very little since the turn of the century was gone for ever.

Yet for many people who came to Feltham in those years, it was a beginning rather than an ending. One resident remembers: 'We lived in London in an upstairs flat with two lively children and no garden and then, in 1950, there was the promise of new houses being built on farmland at the end of Baber Drive. We watched the builders over the months as they put foundations in and houses started to grow. We could walk straight from our new house over the now unused farmland and on to Hounslow Heath and along the Baber Brook, part of the Crane river.

Our garden when we moved in was a field of knee high lush grass left over from the cows on Sparrow Farm. The children could hide if not willing to come in to meals or bed. They spent all that summer building camps in the woods and, we learned later, trying to dam the Baber!

Within the year Sparrow Farm and some adjoining scrubland was bought by the Council and a large housing estate built with roads and shops and our direct access to the Heath was fenced off. Soon there were too many cars for the small roads – but perhaps some of the families on the estate had

Feltham as it looked in 1950

also come from upstairs flats and needed to share the space and freedom with us.'

Part of Feltham is built on land which was once part of the Hanworth estate. Alfred Road and Lafone Avenue are named after the owner of the estate. Where Lafone Avenue is now, there used to be a drive of magnificent horse chestnut trees onto the estate. The surrounding areas were market gardens and orchards. Hanworth Park Court at the top of Alfred Road was built on the site of an early Victorian house with large grounds and Fredellen Maisonettes are on the site of the old coach house of the mansion. Horseshoes have been found in the gardens and the remains of old pipes quite deep in the ground. Underneath the maisonettes are deep stone cellars.

Field End ✺

This pretty corner of Eastcote was, as its name suggests, a small cluster of dwellings standing at the end of open fields. The beginnings of a small community occurred in 1527 when Ralph Hawtrey came from Chequers, married a local girl and founded a family which was centred at Eastcote House.

Field End Road, for its three miles, wends its busy way flanked on either side by well kept dwellings and leafy trees and serves the attractive suburb of Eastcote. At the southern end it spreads tributaries to South Harrow, South Ruislip and Northolt, then goes in its own right westward through Eastcote, curling its way to the half mile at its northern end which is the old Field End. It reaches the junction at Old Eastcote where it spills its busy traffic westward to Ruislip and north-east to Pinner Green.

Back in the mists of time this road was a narrow track which straggled through arable land and pastures, muddy in winter, swirling with dust clouds in hot summers, between the small settlements which dotted its length. Just a handful of farms and clusters of cottages housed the families who worked the land. It remained for hundreds of years a rural community until the coming of the Metropolitan Railway. In 1906 the Eastcote Halt came into being, bringing with it day trippers from London who loved this quiet backwater with its leafy lanes and quiet life style. In the fullness of time there was an influx of new settlers and new homes were built.

The Field End that emerged appears to have been a corner of middle class comfort, and remains so to this present day.

The 16th century Barn House was originally a barn attached to Field End Farm. It has been renovated and serves the community once more, now as offices. Field End Farm has been modernized, although parts remain which date from the 16th century. From 1902 it served as a large dairy farm, the first in this area to deliver milk in bottles. The earliest records show that in 1565 a miller, one John Ferne, owned a house on this site. A story has been handed down through the centuries that in the early 1700s a green light would be hung outside the farmhouse each night as darkness fell, as a warning to wayfarers that to proceed any further was dangerous – evil men were abroad! Perhaps sanctuary was given if needed.

Orchard Farm was built as a cottage in the mid 19th century. It is modernized but its setting suggests the rural life. Within living memory Field End was a narrow lane hosting two large ponds. On what used to be one of the ponds are the Memorial Gardens. Standing in the centre is the war memorial which was moved up from the junction with Bridle Road, as it fell victim many a time in the 1920s to a charabanc which plied its route to Pinner.

Standing back from the road, and a joy to behold, is Tudor Lodge Hotel (once known as Field End Lodge), a timber framed Tudor farmhouse. In 1565 a John Nicholas dwelt here, and it remained a farmhouse until 1873. The building was added to in 1912 and during the First World War it was converted into a VAD hospital, staffed mostly by local girls. A lady in black reputedly walks a corridor which runs across the kitchen area toward the old VAD hospital building. She disappears upon being challenged! Waitresses are aware of a strong perfume pervading the dining room first thing in the morning, and an unexplained warmth emanates from a mirror hanging in the original part of the room. Upstairs strange noises are sometimes heard coming from an empty bedroom!

The road downhill was once called Chapel Hill, because the old Wesleyan church was built down here in 1847, now demolished. There are two dentists, a doctor and three places of worship in one half mile. A part barn, part residential building with a full timbered frame construction, known as

The Retreat dates from the late 16th century. Past it are the splendid semi-detached Field End Villas, built c1856 to house the 'professional classes'.

Park Farm across the road, is a beautiful dwelling standing at right angles to the road. Striking in appearance, it is a Tudor building, with the rendering painted white. In 1565 records state that it was the 'Brick Place' of Thomas Wetherly who paid 1,000 bricks as a rent for it. It was used as a farmhouse until the early 1920s. The interior has been modernized and it serves as a comfortable home for the present family who live there. Just below it is the new Methodist church.

At the bottom of the hill where Field End Road ceases to be, looking rather out of place near a busy roundabout is an ancient white gabled building, dating from the 16th century, called 'Eastcote Cottage'. It stands alone now, gone are the stables and large stableyard and flats have been built in their stead.

Forty Hill 🌿

There are several versions of how Forty Hill got its name but some old maps mark 'Four Tree Hill' and it may well have been derived from this.

Although the parish is extensive and includes some 20th century residential areas along both sides of the Great Cambridge Road and some suburban development on the northern fringe of Enfield, Forty Hill village has survived largely because further development to the west has been restricted by what were originally large private or royal estates which still survive as public open spaces or farmland.

Most of the village is strung along a single road stretching northwards from the village green, which is about a mile

The Goat Tavern at Forty Hill

from Enfield. But being cut off from the main road it gives an illusion of isolation.

On the green stands the Goat public house, but this is a modern building by village standards, dating from 1931. It stands on the site of the old village pond which had a smithy nearby and a large chestnut tree on the green outside. It was from here in 1905 or 1906 that a horse-bus took business-men to Enfield station each morning and brought them back in the evening, with trips for those who wanted to go shopping during the day – price 1d or 2d! This was later replaced by the Blue Admiral motor bus.

Overlooking the green are a number of impressive and well-preserved buildings dating back to the beginning of the 18th century and some, a short distance away, which are even older.

Elsynge House was built on the site of the home of William Grindall, tutor to the future Queen Elizabeth I. It takes its name from Elsynge or Enfield Manor which stood near to Maidens Bridge and was a residence of Henry VIII's children. Canister Lodge (built in 1820) was so named because it looked like a tea caddy of that period. Garnault, with its large number of windows, was built just after the repeal of that tax.

The most prominent house takes its name from the village. Sir Nicholas Raynton started building Forty Hall three years before he became Lord Mayor of London in 1632. The design has been attributed to Inigo Jones, but is probably by one of his circle or close followers. It is said to be one of the finest examples in the country of 17th century domestic building and in the house there is a fine portrait of Sir Nicholas by William Dobson, a pupil of Van Dyck and some beautiful plaster work in the Jacobean tradition. Ownership passed down directly or by marriage until 1799 when it was sold to James Meyer. Forty Hall was acquired in 1895 by Mr H. C. Bowles and remained with this family until it was bought by Enfield District in 1951. It is now open to the public and is used for many exhibitions of local and national interest with other activities taking place in the grounds which are beautifully maintained.

Christian Paul Meyer II (grandson of the purchaser of Forty Hall) endowed Jesus Church. Local legend says it was to save his nine children the trouble of walking to St Andrew's, but it is more likely they all went by carriage and that the new church was for the use of his estate workers. The building was originally a chapel of rest for St Andrew's parish church, Enfield. The design is a copy of a church in Tottenham. One Sunday, many years ago, a young lady fainted in church and had to be taken out. When the verger came with a chair and some water, her friend said that it was her own fault for being too tightly laced. The verger said:

'You foolish young woman. You will kill yourself as sure as your name is, whatever it is, squeezing your heart and liver like that'.

C. P. Meyer II provided a vicarage and his son, James Meyer II, financed Maidens Bridge infant school. The boys were provided with red and blue plaid scarves and the girls had blue capes with red lined hoods. The school closed after Mr Meyer's death.

Forty Hill School, the oldest junior school in Enfield, was opened in 1851. One winter day the master of the school let the boys go out to slide on the gravel pit to get themselves warm; another day boys and girls went out to watch the local hunt and those who failed to return to school were caned the next day!

Opposite Forty Hall is the Clock House which was owned by Mr A. S. Hollington, who had a palmarium made from part of the old Whitechapel railway station. He had extensive gardens and glasshouses in which he grew exotic fruit which he sold locally to finance this hobby. The house was turned into flats in the 1920s and the gardens are now run as Clock House Nursery.

The area is well known for its horticultural interests. Myddelton House (which was named after the builder of the New river which took drinking water from Amwell, in Hertfordshire, to London) was owned in the latter part of the last century by E. A. Bowles who not only encouraged local unemployed youths to learn to read and write, but also to appreciate nature. The house is now the headquarters of the Lee Valley Regional Park Authority. The beautiful grounds are sometimes open to the public. Nearby is Capel Manor Horticultural and Environmental Centre, which is of national importance as a study centre for horticulture and countryside crafts for both amateurs and professionals.

Frances Perry, whose name is always linked with gardening articles and books, grew up in the local pub. The Pied

Bull dates back to the 17th century, when it was kennels for hunting dogs used on the Chase. A deed for 1790 shows that it was a pub by that time. In the bar is an old photograph of children standing round a maypole in the school grounds – a May Day activity vividly remembered by some older villagers.

Another pub in the area is the King and Tinker dating back to Jacobean times. When James VI of Scotland was riding south to become James I of England, a group of people assembled to meet him and a tinker enquired how he would recognise the King. A stranger assured him that everyone else would remove his hat. On looking round the tinker saw everyone bareheaded except the stranger, so he remarked that one of them must be the King and, as it was not himself, it must be the stranger. The King agreed! The pub is on the edge of Whitewebbs park, part of the old hunting Chase but now used by the public for walking, riding and golf.

Although almost entirely a dormitory area, the centre of the parish has a true village atmosphere with a lively interest and pride in local activities, particularly those with a horticultural bent. These combine to make it a delightful place for residents and visitors alike.

Grange Park 🌿

Grange Park is a small residential area only ten miles from Charing Cross yet enjoying a village atmosphere. The boundaries consist of two golf courses, parks and Green Belt land. A post office and a handful of shops serve the community.

Originally the area was farmland, orchards and woods, once the Home Park to the manor of Enfield, when it was used as an enclosure for the beasts of the hunt – boar, stags etc. In 1578 three men went before the London courts for poaching locally and the cases caused so much public interest

Grange Park

that they formed the subject of the play *The Merry Devils of Edmonton* first performed in 1606 – said to have been written by William Shakespeare but not authenticated.

At some time Home Park was re-named Old Park Grange and developers designated the area Grange Park, naming some of the roads Old Park Avenue, Old Park Ridings and Old Park Grove. In the early 1900s land was acquired for a golf course and Old Park Mansion became the club house. Although altered and enlarged over the years, part of the original building still remains.

In 1908 a few large detached houses were built and

purchased by City merchants and in 1910 when the Great Northern Railway extended the line from Wood Green to Cuffley, developers suggested it would be advantageous to both builders and railway if a station or halt was provided! So, in the 1920s and 1930s a variety of houses were built. Wherever possible trees were not disturbed.

Today the village revolves around the two churches, two Women's Institutes and a thriving Horticultural Association founded in 1940 as a result of the 'Dig for Victory' campaign with a membership of 500 and holding very successful annual shows. Youth clubs have come and gone, but Guides and Scouts continue to flourish, several Queen's Awards having been gained over the years.

The parish church of St Peter was dedicated in 1927 but, with the growing number of residents, larger premises were needed and today's church was planned in 1939. Much of the fabric and contents came from London churches destroyed in the Blitz, including roof timbers from many churches and the bell dated 1785 from St John's, Drury Lane. The completed church was consecrated in 1941.

The Methodist church was built in an orchard and so came to be known as 'the Church in the Orchard'. In 1988 it celebrated 50 years in the present building. The original church, now part of the halls, was erected in 1921.

Steam and diesel have come and gone, now electric trains get villagers to London in under 30 minutes. For many years they enjoyed the services of George, the porter, who could be heard some distance away announcing the train's arrival at 'Grange Park', slamming the doors and blowing his whistle. When not engaged in railway duties he retired to his hut and knitted socks! Returning home late at night from London it was advisable to tell the engine driver and guard of your destination as trains were – and still are – sometimes not scheduled to stop at the halt.

The rag and bone man still does his rounds on a Tuesday.

In the days of the horse and cart 6d was the going rate for a bundle of rags and ½d for a jam jar – today he is mechanised and deals mostly in scrap metal.

Further Education classes cater for all ages. The Residents Association has a membership of 900, monthly community lunches provide companionship as well as a meal and Neighbourhood Watch gives a sense of security. At one time a taxi would run to the local hospital from the nearest bus route – now there is a small bus which keeps people in touch with larger shopping precincts nearby.

Sadly the nightingale is no longer heard, but the owl is still around and many beautiful birds visit the gardens as do squirrels and foxes. A small deer has been seen recently enjoying a meal of rosebuds and a pair of herons flying over the brook, no doubt looking for a garden pond with goldfish!

Greenford ❧

> 'And from Greenford scent of mayfields
> Most enticingly was blown.'
>
> Sir John Betjeman.

Greenford means 'the green fields near a ford'. Since Roman times the soil has been known to be suited to wheat growing. The quality of wheat grown in the Greenford area was such that centuries later Elizabeth I commanded it to be supplied to the Royal Household.

Greenford as a village existed before the Norman Conquest – the first written reference is to 'Grenan forda' in AD 845. It is described in the Domesday Book (1086) when most of the land belonged to Westminster Abbey.

The earliest recorded rector is Radbert de Saleby in 1326. The best known is Edward Betham who in 1780 founded the school that still bears his name. Betham Clock School was founded nearly a century later, in 1878. Since 1700 King's College, Cambridge, has had the patronage of the living.

A new church was begun in 1939 but the old church of the Holy Cross still stands. The old church has been rebuilt and altered many times. It was rebuilt at the end of the 15th century and most of the oldest surviving parts of the building date from this period. The building is constructed of flint with stone dressing. There is no stone wall at the west end, instead there is a timber framed and wood-planked tower. The roofs of the nave and chancel are tiled; the tower is covered with oak shingles.

Two boards with the Ten Commandments painted on them originally hung above the chancel arch but are now

Greenford as it looked about 1920

part of the reredos behind the altar. The last major restoration took place in the 1950s. In the chancel window there is stained glass, mostly dating from the 16th century and at some time brought to Greenford from King's College, Cambridge. It is interesting to note in one the old 'peg and post' type of windmill, a type used by the miller of Perivale who appears in the popular legend of the miser robbed by Simon Coston.

The story is that the mill was haunted by a miller and the witch who had cursed him. The witch had fallen to her death from the mill ladder and the miller had been found crushed to death between his own millstones. Some time after these terrible happenings the ruined mill was bought by an old miser. When he had not been seen for some time, the villagers became worried. None of them was brave enough to enter the mill to look for the old man, so they induced young Simon Coston to go – he was a foundling and could not plead family responsibilities to excuse himself! Coston entered the mill and a few moments later rushed out onto the gallery crying 'The ghost! Flee for your lives!' Which they did. However some hours and much ale later, some of the villagers crept back to the mill to see if anything remained of the miser and young Coston. They found the dead body of the old miser – but there was no trace, then or ever, of Simon Coston, or of the miser's gold!

On Saturday 13th November 1937 at 7.30 pm, Gracie Fields opened the Super Grenada Cinema. The film shown was Alice Faye in *Wake up and Live* followed by Claire Trevor and Lloyd Nolan in *King of Gamblers*. Dudley Bevan, ace radio organist, took his place at the Mighty Wurlitzer! Admission prices began at 9d. The cinema was built on the site of an old Roman Catholic church and closed in 1966. The following year a Tesco supermarket was opened on the site of the cinema. The old cinema doors are still retained at the back of the store.

Greenford Hall was purpose-built in 1963 on a farmland site of the old village days and many activities now take place there.

The community centre in Oldfield Lane is of 18th century origin. The manor house was first mentioned in 1305 and called Manor Hall in 1538. The manor courts for Greenford and Hanwell were held here until the two villages separated towards the end of the 17th century.

The Second World War and financial restrictions saved the house from being demolished and gave way to a war-time community centre being set up for the distribution of ration books, identity cards, etc and as a place where the community could go for help and advice. The house reverted back to a community centre after the war and now affords a meeting place for over 60 clubs and organisations.

A familiar sight in Greenford Broadway is the brightly-coloured stall of flowers and plants run by the Fuller family.

When 'Granny Fuller' died, the roads in the Greenford area were lined with people paying their respects to a grand old lady as the cortege passed on its way to Greenford Park Cemetery.

Three generations ago, in the early 1800s, when Greenford was a pretty country village, the flower trade began with a flower basket stand outside a row of cottages. As Greenford grew into a town, the lady trader (Mrs Fuller's mother) moved her pitch to the other side of the road and became established on a spot outside a corn chandler and grocer's shop called Sanders. By now 'Granny' Fuller had taken over from her mother and was gradually joined by her own growing family of son and daughters. Whatever the weather, summer or winter, the family have always been busy selling their flowers and plants until the present day. Customers always receive a cheery greeting and enquiries after their families.

Halliford 🍃

Not many villages can boast of having a holy man. Legend has it that in Anglo-Saxon times a hermit lived in the area by the ford and performed miracles, hence the name Holy Ford, from which the name Halliford has evolved.

Within walking distance of the meandering river Thames, Halliford was, however, inhabited long before the holy man graced it with his presence. The Romans, under Julius Caesar, fought a battle here in 54 BC according to local legend. The river has always been a focal point of life in the area and in the 13th and 14th centuries barges carried wheat, barley and root crops harvested from the lush lands.

It was at about this time that Upper and Lower Halliford emerged and several famous people have since lived in the cluster of houses near Lower Halliford Green. Poets and writers have included Thomas Love Peacock, George Meredith, Rider Haggard and Shelley. None of these, hopefully, ever felt threatened by the gibbet which once stood on the green and until 1810 was housed in the nearby old coach house, although perhaps it somewhat dampened the ardour of Lady Hamilton, who is reputed to have stayed at Halliford and had trysts with Lord Nelson in their favourite local haunts! Royalty has also been associated with the village: King Edgar in AD 963 gave lands to Westminster Abbey at 'Haleghfort'; Queen Elizabeth I held Halliford in 1565; King Charles I's wife Henrietta Maria was given the manor in 1637 and Catherine, the wife of Charles II, held the manor in 1680.

Over the years Halliford has grown beyond recognition, but has still managed to retain its rural aspect. The rich soil and verdant pastures have always attracted people to work on the land and in the late 17th century Huguenots, fleeing from religious persecution in France, planted mulberry trees here in order to continue their silk weaving craft. Alas, the only weaving nowadays is the spider's web, dewdrop-jewelled in the hedgerows, over which cattle poke their heads on misty autumn mornings. But although housing estates have been built on some of the fields and gardening centres have replaced market gardens, buttercups still sprinkle the hedgerows in spring, wild roses bloom in June, corn is harvested in August and there is a profusion of blackberries to be gathered in September.

Up to 50 years ago, Halliford was still a very small village, comprising the manor house, two or three farmhouses and a few cottages. Despite the more recent population explosion, it has managed to retain its village atmosphere, although quite a few of its inhabitants now work further afield at Heathrow airport and some commute to London from the little local station of Halliford Halt – which was constructed during the Second World War for the workers at the nearby British Thermostat factory.

The village community spirit has been greatly fostered by the retention of the local health clinic as a community centre, built on the site of an old chapel. In no small way was this attributable to the Women's Institute, which first started its life in the small reading room of the little village church (a sister church of St Mary's at Sunbury).

There is a village green, where until a short while ago a fair was held on 13th May every year and the WI 'Afternoon on the Green' was held in June. At the turn of the century, Halliford could boast of four inns within half a mile, The Goat, North Star, Halfway House and The Bugle. Only two now remain, The Goat and The Bugle. The Goat is thought to be about 200 years old and was in the beginning a small, single-bar beer house with a sawdust strewn floor. After the Second World War, there was often a shortage of beer and when hostelries ran out in Walton-on-Thames or Sunbury, for example, the drinkers would move down to Halliford to see if they had stocks, but The Goat's formidable landlord reserved what beer he had for his regular village drinkers! Since about 1950, the beer house has been built on and extended until now it is the present rambling Goat Inn.

The river and its wildlife remains a constant source of pleasure – Halliford bend is mentioned in *Three Men in a Boat*. There is much emphasis on water in the adjoining area with gravel pits and reservoirs. An old notice on the bridge at Halliford (unfortunately now gone) told what might have happened if you damaged it –

'Any person wilfully injuring any part of this County Bridge will be guilty of FELONY and upon Conviction be liable to be kept in PENAL SERVITUDE FOR LIFE

by the court

24th and 25th Vic. Cap 97.   Richard Nicholson'

Maybe this would be the answer to today's vandalism!

Hampton-on-Thames

There was a parish of Hampton in Anglo-Saxon times, the name deriving from the Anglo-Saxon words meaning 'the settlement in the bend of the river'. This describes the village's position at the western end of the big bend in the river Thames which circles the present Hampton Court Home Park on three sides.

The records show vicars of St Mary's church back to 1342 and the church was probably in existence before then. The older church was enlarged in 1679 and in 1726 when a north aisle and schoolroom were added. The old church was pulled down in 1829 and replaced by the present one which was consecrated in 1831. The medieval church dominated the river and ferry and the older houses were gathered round it, the vicarage and the vicar's glebe barn and the 17th century taverns. Still today the finest view of Hampton is to be seen from the southern, Molesey side of the Thames across to the church and buildings along the river bank.

The easy river communications with London and the ancient great pastures of Hampton were important influences on local economic life long before the palace came. Thames fishermen and watermen kept the weirs, worked the ferries, tended the osier beds and manned the barges. Basket making was a local industry and the osier beds by the ferry and on the ait now known as Tagg's Island survived into the early 19th century. The first bridge at Hampton Court was not built until 1753 so the Hampton ferries were an important feature until that time.

Cardinal Thomas Wolsey acquired land at Hampton Court in 1514. He was already the most powerful and richest subject in the kingdom and he proceeded to build and furnish his country house on the bank of the Thames with a magnificence rivalling, if not surpassing, that of a royal palace. His household numbered nearly 500 and 280 richly furnished rooms were kept always prepared for guests, but his fall was near. In 1529 he was stripped of all his wealth and power. In a desperate effort to regain the King's favour he presented to Henry VIII his manor of Hampton Court with its buildings and furnishings, tapestries and plate but on 30th October 1529 all his lands and goods were declared forfeit to the King and he died soon after, a broken man.

King Henry VIII at once began to enlarge the house, making it one of the most luxurious palaces in the kingdom. The second great rebuilding at Hampton Court took place during the reign of William and Mary, who commissioned Sir Christopher Wren to rebuild the State rooms and private apartments of the Sovereign. After the death of George II in 1760, the palace was never again occupied by a reigning monarch and Queen Victoria opened the State Rooms to the public. The maze was planted in the reign of Queen Anne and is still one of the most popular features of the gardens. The close-clipped hedges which line the paths are six ft high and two ft thick.

The building of Hampton Court Palace undoubtedly led to an upturn in the local economy, creating both employment and the growth of inns and shops.

During many outbreaks of plague in London in the 16th and 17th centuries, the Court fled to Hampton Court and other wealthy Londoners followed the Court's example and established country houses or cottages in Hampton. So 400 years ago Hampton was something of a commuter town, although nothing like the scale on which it is today! The Manor Books of the late 17th century mention many cottages, some detached or some in rows and all had their stables and land of orchards and gardens attached.

The present vicarage, built in 1883, stands on an ancient vicarage site; alongside stood Hamonde's schoolhouse, the forerunner of the present Hampton School, an independent boys grammar school. To one side stood the 16th century Bell Inn, the income from which was bequeathed by Robert Hamonde to endow Hampton School. The present Bell Inn, built in 1893, stands on the same site. On the other side of the church and vicarage stand three old cottages. The centre one called today the Feathers Cottage bears a name well known in Hampton for over 300 years, for in the 17th century the whole block was the Feathers Inn. Beyond the Bell was the Shipp Tavern, on the site of the modern 20th century Red Lion. Sir Christopher Wren dined there as a guest of the parish when he came to see the new church steeple in 1679. A nearby cottage, now an Italian restaurant, still incorporates some of the 17th century structure.

Along the river bank stood several large houses, including St Albans, The Cedars and Hampton House. The last two came into the possession of the famous actor David Garrick in the mid 18th century and were renamed Garrick's Lodge and

Garrick's Villa. Both these houses have fortunately been preserved, Garrick's Villa with its handsome portico front having been converted into very elegant and expensive flats. Modern Georgian style town houses have been built in the grounds forming Hogarth Way and Johnsons Drive (after Dr Samuel Johnson who often visited David Garrick). The elegant Garrick's Temple, erected by him in 1757, still stands in the public gardens along the river bank.

No such happy fate befell St Albans. This house had a fascination for Hamptonians because of the unfounded myth that it had been built for Charles II to house his mistress Nell Gwynne, the mother of the first Duke of St Albans. The house actually took its name from the 5th Duke of St Albans who lived there after his country seat Hanworth Park was destroyed by fire in 1797. The last owner of St Albans, Theodore Cory, who died in 1961, left the house to the borough for public use as a meeting place, lecture hall or museum, but there was no money for its upkeep and after years of indecision, the house began to collapse and was demolished in 1972.

A similar fate awaited Spring Grove, a mid-18th century house which took its name from the spring which was the original source of water for Hampton Court Palace. The last owner, Dr Foss, died in 1971. Nothing was done by the Court of Protection to preserve the house which finally disintegrated and was demolished in 1981; 15 terrace houses now stand on the site.

Running north from the river lay the 18th century manor house, demolished in 1938 to make way for the Manor building estate. Tagg's Island which lies in the Thames at Hampton, was named after a boat builder Mr Tagg, who built an hotel on the island in 1873. The hotel was taken over by Fred Karno and renamed The Karsino. The renown of the Karsino faded after the First World War. The hotel continued as The Casino for some years – a Palm Court type of hotel where companies held their annual dinner-dances. The island was eventually taken over by the Tagg's Island Trust which sold long leases of the mooring plots to the island residents. The comedienne sisters Elsie and Doris Waters lived for many years on a houseboat moored at Tagg's Island.

Before the end of the 19th century, Hampton was developing to the north-west where much of the former farmland was converted to market gardens and nurseries. The expansion resulted in the formation of another parish, that of All Saints, with a new church consecrated in 1908. Before the 1970s the glasshouses were counted in hundreds and provided employment for many Hampton residents, but the number of nurseries fell from 48 in 1912 to eight in 1973. The 1970s and 1980s have seen an enormous change in which about one quarter of Hampton's area has been transformed from one of the largest market garden areas in Middlesex into a housing estate, 'The Nurserylands'. Hampton Residents Association has been active in achieving a suitable balance between council, private and Housing Association building and the provision of community services, open spaces and playing fields.

It is almost 100 years since Henry Ripley in his *History and Topography of Hampton-on-Thames* wrote 'the building interests have fixed their eyes upon its pleasant meads and shady lanes' but he could not have foreseen that by the present day there would be no land remaining for another housing estate, assuming that land hitherto considered inviolable – schoolfields, public parks, recreation grounds and allotments remain so!

Hampton residents are proud that they fought for and still have their own cottage hospital, St Mary's and part of old Hampton has been designated a conservation area. Many plans have been suggested to divert heavy traffic from the oldest part in Thames Street. The traffic problem was made worse with the completion of the M3 at Sunbury but was alleviated to some extent, with regard to heavy lorries in particular, by the opening of the M25. Quite a different sort of traffic problem is the noise from aircraft flying over Hampton. What a change from the gentle lapping of the water round the boats on the Thames which brought the 16th century residents to Hampton!

Hanwell 🌿

Hanwell owes its development to river, road and rail. Several Stone and Bronze Age implements have been found in the area and in 1886 the graves of ten 6th century West Saxon warriors were excavated from a gravel pit on the site of the present Oaklands school.

The name Hanewelle (meaning a 'cock-frequented spring') does not appear until AD 959 when Alfwyn, the lord of the manor, pawned Hanwell in exchange for £30 in silver from the Archbishop of Canterbury so that he could make a pilgrimage to Rome. He returned penniless, unable to redeem his pledge, but the Archbishop allowed him to remain on the estate until his death when he gave the land to the monastery of St Peter in Westminster.

In 1484 William Hobbayne bequeathed his farm to the parish for 'godly purposes'. It consisted of a house and 23 acres of land which the Hobbayne Charity trustees sold or leased over the years to provide funds for the poor or the maintenance of the church. The charity still owns land in Hanwell and is now 500 years old.

During Elizabethan times the woodlands covering Cuckoo Hill were cleared for growing wheat, but as the number of stagecoaches on the turnpike road to Oxford increased, hayfields began to replace arable land although sheep and cattle were still kept. The river Brent made Hanwell a natural stopping place for coaches. Horses could be watered and rested and the travellers were well provided for by inns like the Coach and Horses (now the Viaduct) which offered overnight shelter from the highwaymen who prowled the lonely heath beyond.

In 1854 the London Poor Law Guardians purchased 112 acres of Cuckoo Farm to build a residential school for the hundreds of children in the workhouses and those who had been orphaned or abandoned. The London District Schools (better known as Cuckoo Schools) opened soon after. Cuckoo Farm and Schools closed in 1933 and by the outbreak of the Second World War the LCC had errected 1,592 houses, two churches and three schools on the 140 acre site. The administration block and clocktower of the old school survive to this day and it is used as a community centre. Charlie Chaplin was a pupil at the old Cuckoo Schools.

Hanwell Preservation Society and the Brent River and Canal Society now protect the older parts of Hanwell and the area surrounding the river Brent.

Hanworth 🦌

One often wonders what Henry VIII would say if he could look down to see the thick-limbed concrete reptile that winds its way all over his beloved Hanworth. To most of the daily commuters on this, the M3 feederway, the village marks just another spot in time on their daily journey to the great metropolis.

Few will ever stop to think, and the majority will never know, that they are travelling over lands where four centuries ago Tudor kings and queens hunted the fleet footed deer, the less renowned wild boar, the darting hare and the fluttering pheasant. For it was to his village, his Hanworth, not four miles distant from Hampton Court, that Henry came with all his courtiers and their servants to hunt on the lands surrounding the manor and its adjacent stables at Tudor Court. The latter, surrounded by a protective moat, is still preserved in part today from the ever growing modernisation of the rural countryside.

Hanworthian history goes back even further than that, for the aforementioned moat is considered to date from Saxon times and the yew tree standing at the door of the parish church of St George is reputed to be over 1,000 years old.

Hanworth manor was mentioned in the Domesday Book as part of the Spelthorne Hundred and its tenure was granted by William the Conqueror to Roger De Montgomery, Earl of Arundel. Mary Tudor was brought up as a child in Hanworth and Elizabeth I spent many happy hours here, hunting. To this day visitors may stand on the stone she used when mounting her horses in the stable yard at Tudor Court. Cardinal Wolsey also made use of Hanworth manor at Henry's invitation to shield him from the great plague of those days. The old manor house was burnt down in 1797 and the new Hanworth House was built by the Duke of St Albans and bought by Henry Perkins, a rich Southwark brewer.

The growth of Hanworth was very slow and in the 18th century the village had only three more houses than in Tudor times – the coming of the railway to nearby Feltham was to alter that!

Hanworth has also played a role in military history. It is recorded that gunpowder, used at the battle of Crecy in 1346 was made and stored in Hanworth. Large factories for the manufacture of gunpowder were established on the banks of the river Crane and successfully operated until 1926.

With the park, Hanworth has also played its part in the history of the aircraft. Planes were built on the estate during both World Wars and in the period between the wars it was a centre for private aviation. Many of the older residents still recall the heady days of 1931–1932 when the mighty German airship, the Graf Zeppelin, visited the park.

Today, Hanworth has turned into a sleepy suburban village, the dormitory of London and nearby Heathrow airport workers – woken for a fortnight each year by the gaiety and laughter of its nationally famous carnival which since its inception 30 years ago, has contributed so much to Cancer Research.

Harefield 🎝

Harefield is situated on a ridge overlooking the Colne valley, in the north-west of Hillingdon Borough, on the borders of Buckinghamshire and Hertfordshire. Because of its isolated position it has remained a separate village with no railway and surrounded by farmland.

The name evolved from Herefelle, which may mean 'an open space where an army camped'. The name is first found in Saxon times, but man was here much earlier, as flints, Neolithic axes and evidence of Iron age occupation have been found. In the Domesday Book it states that the village owner was Richard FitzGilbert. By 1444 the manor had passed to the Newdigate family who had a mansion, Harefield Place at the bottom of the hill, with a church close by. The house has gone but the church still stands, isolated amidst fields. It is frequently used in films. It has a plain exterior but the inside is widely known for its remarkable collection of monuments, many belonging to the Newdigate family, dating from the 15th century.

The most impressive tomb is that of Alice, Countess of Derby, which is richly coloured. This lady's second husband was Sir Thomas Egerton, Lord Keeper of the Great Seal. The Countess lived here from 1601 to 1637. She was a great patron of the Arts and Milton wrote his masque *Arcades* for her. In 1602 Queen Elizabeth I visited Harefield Place, staying three days. This must have been a tremendous event in the village. The Egerton papers recorded that the vast amount of food, entertainments and gifts cost Sir Thomas £4,000. It apparently rained the whole time! The Countess built the almshouses on Church Hill 'for six poor widows' and these are still in use.

Another large estate was 'Breakspears', of which the first known owner was William Breakspear in the 14th century. He may have been from the same family as Nicholas, the only English Pope, who was born not far away in Hertford-shire in the 12th century. In the 1930s this house was sold to the Middlesex County Council. It has been a home for the elderly for some years. There is said to be a blocked up hiding place in the older part of the house and it is known that Sir Robert Ashby concealed priests in 1604. W. S. Gilbert lived in the house for three years and wrote *The Yeoman of the Guard* there.

Harefield Park was owned by an Australian, Mr Billyard Leake in 1915, and he offered the estate to the Australian Government as a hospital for Australian soldiers for the duration of the First World War. Thousands passed through and sadly 111 soldiers and one nursing sister died. A piece of the churchyard was set aside as a burial ground. At the first soldier's funeral the school Union Jack was used to cover the coffin and this was used until after the war, when the flag was sent to Adelaide High School and they sent Harefield school a new one and an Australian flag. In 1921 identical headstones and an obelisk were erected in the graveyard and since then on Anzac Day, April 25th, children from the junior school lay posies of spring flowers on every grave and a service is held. During the Second World War food parcels came to the village from Australia.

The hospital huts were used after the First World War for people suffering from tuberculosis, and in 1937 a new

The Almshouses at Harefield M. Evans.

hospital was built. St Mary's from London came here during the Second World War. Now that TB is largely a disease of the past the hospital has become known world wide for its heart and lung transplants.

Harefield House became the home in the 1920s of Mr H. Avary Tipping, a well known writer on architecture and gardening, and he laid out beautiful grounds. The church fête was held there for many years. When he died he left the bulk of his estate to his head gardener, Mr W. Wood who was a keen cricketer. A cricket field had been laid out on the estate and Mr Wood gave it to the village. It is a lovely spot, surrounded by gardens and trees. Most of the gardens of the house have now gone as the Air Ministry bought the estate and built on it.

Harefield has always been a working village; the estates and farms employed many people, but there has been industry too. The canal came through the valley in 1797 and industry grew up, with brickworks, cement and limeworks for a time. A factory on the site of a cornmill is still being used. However, most of the heavier industry is ceasing and light technology is arriving.

Harefield is in the Green Belt and the Colne Valley Park and the centre of the village is a conservation area. As a result of gravel digging in the Colne valley there is a string of lakes used for leisure pursuits. One of the farms, Park Lodge is run as a centre for school-children from the London boroughs to learn about the countryside, while Knightscote Farm has a museum of farming and a 19th century house is a residential study centre for Inner London primary children.

There are quite a number of small shops and when the 'Co-op' closed down a village committee was formed which, after a lot of hard work and generosity from inhabitants and local businesses, was able to re-open the stores as a village shop for the benefit of the villagers.

There are still a number of old houses and a common and pond in the centre of the village, and thanks to former estates and a policy of new planting, there are many fine trees everywhere.

Harlington

The first record of Harlington appears in the Domesday Book of 1086. Herdintone, as it was then called, was an agricultural area, which consisted of a manor, about 18 freemen, peasants with their families and a priest, although at this stage no mention is made of a church.

This part of the Thames Basin, fertile ground with gravel not far below the surface, was widely used for market gardening, being so near to the big London markets. There were many orchards in the area, the names of some of these still in use in Cherry Lane and Victoria Lane.

Another industry which flourished in the area at one time was brickmaking, and there is still a Brickfield Lane. Then gravel became an important industrial item, and since then the village has suffered considerably from its extraction.

Towards the end of the Second World War much of the agricultural land was taken over to become Heathrow airport. As the airport grew, so did the need for hotels. Now what was once a small village has spread out to almost join neighbouring villages, with just a few fields and areas of closely guarded Green Belt land between.

However the village does still retain the ancient church of St Peter and St Paul, now over 900 years old, a building of great beauty and antiquity. The church is very well worth visiting. Its south door dates from about 1130, the font from about 1190 and there is a Tudor doorway to the clergy vestry. The parish registers begin in 1540. The original oak beams in the roof give a feeling of timelessness and the Easter Sepulchre erected about 1545 is one of the most interesting items in the church, particularly as there are so few of them left in this country.

No record of Harlington would be complete without mention of the Harlington Yew Tree, on the south side of the church. It is believed that the yew is well over 1,000 years old, being here long before the church was built and was possibly the religious meeting place in pagan times.

There used to be a village pond but in the early 1950s this fell into disuse and because it became an eyesore it was filled in and became the present village green, a pleasant place with lawns, trees and seats. One particular tree marks the place where the old village pond used to be. Now once a year, on a Friday evening in late June, on this site, the Village Association organizes a village fair, with everyone joining in the fun. At the moment money raised at this event goes towards funding the Harlington Hospice, the on-going village project. Sadly the cottage hospital has long since been put to other uses.

William Byrd, the composer, lived in Harlington for about 14 years during the reign of Queen Elizabeth I. No trace is left of where he lived, although the most recently opened junior and infant school in the village is called the William Byrd School.

Charles Dickens was a frequent visitor to a house in Hatton Road, now swallowed up by the airport, where the original 'Little Dorrit' lived.

Part of the village High Street was diverted in 1965 when the M4 motorway cut through it, Cherry Lane being slightly re-routed. A small section was called St Paul's Close and the longer section on the far side is now known as Shepiston Lane – Shepiston being the name of one of the manors in the very early records.

The Coach and Horses, the first coaching inn on the London to Bath run was at Harlington Corner and many were the stories of highwaymen (Hounslow Heath was not far off) and of body-snatchers, connected with the ancient hostelry. Alas, with modern progress the old Coach and Horses was pulled down some years ago and the modern circular hotel, the Ariel, erected in its place.

Harmondsworth

Mentioned in the Domesday Book, the village goes back to pre-Roman times. The name is a derivation of two words – Hermode and worth – the latter being Saxon for farm or manor and Hermode, the proper name of some Saxon overlord. No doubt through varied spelling caused by mis-pronunciation, it finally became Harmondsworth.

A well preserved tithe barn still exists, the colossal propor-tions of which make it one of the greatest timber buildings in England. Nearly 200 feet long and 36 feet wide, with

The Great Tithe Barn at Harmondsworth

cathedral-like roof, it has survived virtually intact since the 15th century.

St Mary's church has several notable features. On the outside wall to the right of the porch a mass dial can be seen and there is a fine Norman doorway. The parish registers contain the names of several people who were 'touched for the King's Evil' – an ancient custom going back to the time of Edward the Confessor, when it was believed that a person touched by the sovereign would be cured of scrofula (tuberculosis). The 'touching' probably took place at Windsor and the register was kept to show that the person was 'free from infection'.

The graveyard, shaken every few minutes now by aircraft, contains the graves of Richard Cox, who cultivated the famous Cox's Orange Pippin apple, and Peggy Bedford, for upwards of 50 years the landlady of an inn on the Bath Road known as The King's Head. The name was later changed and the present 'Peggy Bedford' stands at the junction of the Bath Road and the Colnbrook by-pass.

The parish workhouse, which stood on the Bath Road on part of the site on which the Skyway Hotel now stands, housed those on 'in relief'. It was controlled by a workhouse master who was elected annually by the vestry. The physically fit inmates were sent out to work on the local farms, and the wages they earned became the property of the workhouse master, who had to provide their clothes.

Two listed Georgian houses, The Lodge and Harvard House (formerly The Grange) are now business premises, but have been tastefully restored after years of neglect. The blacksmith's forge is now used for light engineering.

The Sun House, once the property of St Mary's church, remains externally much the same as it was in the reign of Queen Elizabeth I. In the past it was an inn and a butcher's shop, the meat hooks still visible today supporting hanging flower baskets. There are now only two pubs in the village, the Five Bells and the Crown.

With the close proximity of Heathrow airport, the village is no longer a sleepy backwater. The bondmen of the Middle Ages, tied to the land and obliged to render to their lord various labour services and levies, have been replaced by present-day commuters, airport and hotel workers and there is a continuous movement in the population.

For almost 60 years the village had a thriving WI which was responsible for much of the social life. Their annual summer fete, always held in the walnut orchard of Manor Farm, was a very popular occasion. The highlight of this event was a display by the volunteer fire brigade, which existed in Harmondsworth from around 1790 until the time of nationalisation. It is believed they kept the fire engine at the parish church. In 1884 the brigade faced its biggest test when fire swept through Harmondsworth village destroying the Baptist church, buildings and houses.

Airport runways, hotels and housing estates have now replaced the once flourishing market gardens, but Harmondsworth is still surrounded by fields.

Harrow on the Hill 🌿

Harrow Hill rises high above the Middlesex plain with the spire of St Mary's church a prominent landmark. It is an area which abounds with historical associations spanning more than a thousand years.

Archbishop Lanfranc began to build the church in 1087 and it was consecrated by his successor St Anselm on 4th January 1094. There is a Norman font, an ancient chest and a door which has been in use for nearly 800 years. The pulpit is 17th century. The roofs of the nave and transepts are said

Harrow on the Hill

to be the finest in Middlesex, they and the spire date from the middle of the 15th century.

The chancel roof was restored in the latter part of the 18th century and painted in 1972. The battlements on the nave roof and the flint facing on the building date from about 1849.

John Lyon, a local farmer who founded the famous Harrow School in 1572, is buried 'near his seat in the church'. There is an interesting inscription on his brass, now on the wall and he is also commemorated on a monument by Flaxman on the wall above the brass. Lord Byron when a boy at Harrow School would spend many hours on the Peachey stone in the churchyard near the terrace. He loved the hilltop and his little daughter Allegra is buried in an unmarked grave outside the church door.

An upright slate tombstone inscribed with an amusing verse commemorates Thomas Port, probably the first person to be killed by a train on the original Euston to Manchester line which runs through Wealdstone, at that time, 1838, within the old parish of Harrow.

Harrow was also the scene of the first fatal car crash. The car overturned at the foot of Grove Hill killing one man and fatally injuring another. A tablet commemorating this accident is fixed to the wall at the top of Grove Hill.

On Church Hill leading up to St Mary's a plaque set high on the wall commemorates Anthony Ashley Cooper who later became the 7th Earl of Shaftesbury. While a boy at Harrow he saw two men carrying a pauper's coffin to the churchyard from the old workhouse (now number 35 West Street). The men had been paid in advance to carry it and had got drunk on the money. They were staggering all over the road laughing and joking. Just as they reached the boy they dropped the coffin. They picked it up with much swearing and cursing. The awful scene made such an impression on Anthony Ashley Cooper that he resolved to devote his life to help the poor and underprivileged.

The double fronted building on the left as one walks up Church Hill is known as the Old School of Harrow School. The left or east side was the original schoolroom which was begun in 1608 and opened in 1615. It was built to fulfil the instructions of the school's founder John Lyon after the death of his wife Joan in 1608. Many subsequently famous men carved their names on the panels of the room while they were at school including Lord Byron; Robert Peel, Prime Minister and founder of the Metropolitan Police; Fox Talbot, the inventor of the photographic negative; Lord Palmerston; Sheridan the dramatist; Trollope the novelist and many others.

The school house known as the Headmaster's which stands opposite the bottom of Church Hill replaced the original house which was burnt down in 1839. The fire started in a defective hot air heating system. Eyewitnesses tell of the valiant efforts made by the boys to save the house. They formed one line along the High Street to The Park garden where there was a pond and a second line up Church Hill to another pond in The Grove garden. The boys passed buckets of water along these human chains. Meanwhile the Harrow fire engine pumped frantically, but the firemen were dismayed that no water came. They found that vandals had cut the pipes and all the water was running away down West Street. By the time fire engines had come from London it was too late to save the Headmaster's. So the Housemaster of Druries, the house opposite, bribed the firemen to play their hoses on his house instead as he feared that sparks and flames from across the narrow street would ignite it.

At the top of Grove Hill there is a spot known as King Charles' Well. Today no well is visible but King Charles I stopped to water his horses there whilst fleeing from the Parliamentary army to the protection, as he thought, of the Scottish army who had promised him safe conduct. Whilst he watered his horse King Charles looked sadly from Grove Hill towards the London he thought he would never see again. But he did! The Scottish army sold King Charles back to the Parliamentarians who eventually beheaded him at Whitehall.

Many other famous church people as well as Archbishop Lanfranc and St Anselm have Harrow connections. Thomas a Becket, St Thomas of Canterbury, was at Harrow ten days before Christmas 1170. He returned to Canterbury and on Christmas Day, four days before his martyrdom, excommunicated the rector of Harrow for cutting off the tail of one of his horses and shooting arrows at him from the church-tower as he left for Canterbury.

The Hill is the oldest part of the large borough of Harrow which was sparsely inhabited until the coming of the railway. Many old farms have been swept away to make room for modern shops and houses but Headstone Manor, a moated house dating from the 14th century, remains. At one time a manor of the Archbishops of Canterbury and the oldest continuously inhabited house in Middlesex, it may be visited, as well as the tithe barn and Heritage Centre nearby.

Harrow Weald ℘

The Weald or Wold once spread across the northern part of Middlesex and, consisting of dense woodland, probably remained uninhabited for many years. There was a track from London, leading along Kenton Lane, up Clamp Hill to Old Redding and thence to St Albans. The Romans may have had the Mount built as a lookout, southwards, but Bell Mount (Belmont) began as a wooded knoll.

Saxon farmers began felling trees to allow the cultivation of the land. Oak trees were felled for boat and house building, while the wood was also used for charcoal burning. By the Domesday survey of 1086, within the boundaries of the parish of Harrow were the hamlets of Pinner, Roxeth, Preston, Kenton, Wembley and Weald (Harrow Weald). Fitz-stephen, the chronicler, described in 1180 the beautiful woods and groves of the Weald. The concealed wild game, stags, boars and bulls, which provided good hunting for lords of the manor.

In the mid 15th century Harrow Weald was known as the 'Welde', from the Old English meaning a woodland. There were a few groups of thatched cottages and narrow, un-kempt tracks bordered by grass verges. Four tithingmen were allocated, which suggests a total population of about 160, plus the various members of the lord of the manor's staff. The theft of deer from private parks or cattle from meadows was a serious offence, the sentence then being to be 'skinned like a live eel', doubtless resulting in death!

From early in the 13th century Bentley Priory exerted a monastic influence in the area. Bentley is an old Anglo-Saxon word meaning 'a place on a hill covered with coarse grass'. The Archbishop demanded an annual rent of 5/2½d and a priest was appointed to say the weekly mass. When he fell down on his duties, the priory fell into disuse. It passed through many hands until finally wealthy James Duberly demolished the priory and built the existing house.

The extensive woodland was mainly of oak. A special keeper was employed to see that swine owners paid 'pannage', or one penny for each pig that searched the woods for acorns. This enabled the lord of the manor to have an income, from this source, of about 35 shillings a year. Oaks were requisitioned by Henry VIII to roof his chapel at Westminster and also to build the navy's fleet of warships.

Of 22 private estates, 14 have been demolished and one, Woodlands, vandalised. Those remaining are Grimsdyke, The Kiln, Tanglewood, Glenthorne, Cottesmore, Harrow Weald Lodge and Harrow Weald House.

Here as elsewhere during the 19th century, poorer folk did not fare well. Drinking water was often foul and, being of weakened health, many died from tuberculosis, cholera and rickets. A survey of 119 people buried in Harrow Weald churchyard between 1847 and 1856, found that the average age at death was 29.5 years.

The Colne Valley Water Company installed piped water for Harrow Weald in 1876. Prior to 1914 few terraced houses and cottages had bathrooms and water closets were outside in a wooden shelter, with no facilities for flushing water. Modernisation began between the 1920s and 1930s. Residential areas were built in avenues, closes, rows, ways, drives or lanes. Heavy clay ground hampered progress but, as the railways advanced, commuting to work became possible and families moved further out from London. Market gardening and plant nurseries were replaced by smoke free, modern factories.

Under the Amalgamation of Railways Act of 1921, railwaymen from Manchester (London and York Railway), Derby (Midland Railway) and Stoke on Trent (Northern and Scottish) were moved to offices in London and were amongst the earliest residents in the 1930s on the New College estate.

In the 15th century this land had belonged to Richard Walworth and about a hundred years later, in 1504, Sherborne Langton presented the land to New College, Oxford. To help offset financial problems, New College began selling off the estate in 1926. Richard Goddard, the last farmer, vacated the farmhouse where he had lived with his two sisters. The buildings were destroyed by fire in the early 1930s.

The estate was bought by John Searcy, FAI and he built 16 houses to the acre in 1933. It is said that bricks for Hibbert Road were made by Searcy's men in a shed located in Fisher Road. The window frames were manufactured in Russia! Much business was thought to go on in the Duck In The Pond, where Bill Colwell was publican.

The Bishop of Willesden contacted John Searcy about the need for a new church in the fast growing community. As a result of this Searcy presented the site for Wykenham Hall and St Michael's and All Angels church, at the end of Bishop Ken Road (named after Thomas Ken, Bishop of Bath and Wells in the 17th century).

1933 was an exceptionally warm summer, which caused the plaster in the new houses to dry too quickly and young trees to die, but eventually tree lined roads were established on the new estate. Many of them were named after students or tutors closely associated with New College.

Contrary perhaps to expectations, the nearby College Avenue, College Hill Road and College Road were so named because of their proximity to the Rev Munro's College of St Andrew, which has not survived. The houses were built mainly in the late 1920s and early 1930s. College Avenue boasts one splendid house built in 1934 for Dr Hammond. Called 'Green Mouton', it resembles the current Odeon cinemas.

It is interesting to look back at the amenities considered modern in those new terraced houses of the 1930s. Each house had lead-piped water to kitchen and upstairs bathroom, with separate flushing lavatory. A kitchen coke boiler supplied hot water. There were gas fires in the walls of two bedrooms and a gas point in the small bedroom, both downstairs rooms and kitchen. The kitchen was 'furnished' with a modern Hygena cabinet complete with flour sifter, a gas washing boiler, large stone sink and one electric point for an electric iron. The shopping list indicator inside the cabinet door 'brings joy to the home' and listed items such as ammonia, blue, candles, firewood, platepowder, gravy browning, tapioca, turpentine and whiting (for cleaning canvas tennis shoes)!

In the 1930s it was possible to walk along hedge-lined Kenton Lane and Clamp Hill to Old Redding. From there was an expansive view southwards to Harrow Hill, South Harrow, Horsenden Hill and around. Happily today there is still the same view of the countryside, with the viewpoint increased to a large car park and a safe grassed playing area, with horses nearby, and often magnificent sunsets.

Behind is Harrow Weald common land and Grimsdyke (now a hotel), where W. S. Gilbert lived and very sadly died. He worked hard to maintain the common around his house, causing the Act of 1899 to be passed and this is displayed at entrances to the common.

Further along Old Redding at The Kiln are remnants of the brick and tile kilns of Charles Blackwell. Originally the works were developed by the Bodimeade family in the 17th century. It was a relative of Charles Blackwell who, in 1829, began a partnership with Edmund Crosse, forming the Crosse and Blackwell Company.

Gravel from pits on Harrow Weald common was used to surface the newly made roads and is occasionally visible during repairs, as it is now below the modern tarmacadam. At first streets were lit by electricity, but the council found this too expensive and it was changed to gas. A lamplighter would come round with his ladder and cycle from lamp to lamp. Often at lighting-up time, in winter, the muffin man would come by, ringing his bell and carrying the muffins, covered with a cloth and in a basket, on a board balanced on his cloth cap.

Hatch End ✑

As a name Hatch End has been in use for many hundreds of years. Indeed, from documents preserved in the Middlesex Records, it would appear that in 1448, Hatch End was 'le Hacchehend', meaning the district by the gate. Some say this was a gate of Pinner Park, some say it was a gateway to Windsor Forest.

Grim's Dyke earthwork, now still an earthwork of major importance in the county, is four miles long and runs through parts of Hatch End. Several sugestions have been made as to the origin of this earthwork and its name. According to *Place-Names of Middlesex* Grim is probably another word for the god Woden, to whose activities these ancient earthworks were attributed. However, it is quite obvious that at some unspecified date this great barrier was set up by human agency and the only certainty is that it is of pre-Norman origin.

Until very recently Hatch End was a completely rural area. As well as the seven large farms, there were numerous smallholdings from the 16th to the 19th centuries, some of them still working farms today. These farms employed many agricultural labourers and domestic servants, many of whom came from Ireland.

By 1861 the type of community had changed. Between 1851 and 1861 50 houses were built and were inhabited, including the pub. These people were newcomers who had nothing to do with agriculture – barristers, surgeons, clergymen etc.

One such family lived at 2 Chandos Villas: the Beetons. Samuel Beeton was a publisher from London and his wife, Isabella, compiled her famous *Book of Household Management* at this house. In the winter of 1858 she ran a soup kitchen for the families of local agricultural labourers, employing her recipe 'Useful Soup for Benevolent Purposes'.

Although a gas supply was introduced in the 1860s, householders had to rely on wells and other sources of water until a piped supply was laid on in the 1880s.

In 1585, a Joan Barringer of Harrow Weald appeared before the Middlesex Justice of the Peace, accused of causing the death of Rose Edlyn, of Hatch End, by witchcraft. The Edlyn family lived at 'Parke Gate' which may be identified with Hatch End Farmhouse, now Letchford House, the oldest house in Hatch End and well preserved in character.

Hatch End railway station opened in 1911 (the first passenger train on the London/Birmingham railway ran through Hatch End in 1837). It replaced the old Pinner Station dating from 1844. The station has been described as one of the few really good minor stations in Greater London.

Essentially a middle class area, Hatch End did not develop in the same way as other villages. As late as 1910 there were still no shops in the village, but with the opening of the station many houses were built, and shops were soon to follow. In 1914 a motor bus was provided by the railway company to replace the horse-drawn omnibus which connected Hatch End with Pinner village.

Hatch End parish church of St Anselm was consecrated in 1895 – a lovely church, the proudest possession of which is its oak open-work rood screen, filling the whole of the chancel arch. Permission to erect this screen was refused at first because the Low Church party objected, but with local support an appeal was made, the previous decision was overruled and the screen was later dedicated by the Bishop of London. Of interest, too, are several lovely windows designed by a local man, Louis Davis.

Although Hatch End has grown in the past few years, it still retains a village atmosphere. Famous residents of the village have included A. E. Housman, author of *A Shropshire Lad* and Jessie Mathews, the popular actress and singer of the 1920s and 30s. Rebecca West, the writer and friend of H. G. Wells, brought up their son in Hatch End.

Hayes

The village of Hayes was called 'Cotman's Town' in 1598 and appears to have been grouped around the church. In 1929 there is a reference in a Court Book to 'Hayes Town formerly called Cotman's Town'. Hayes or Hesa as it was known is however mentioned in the Domesday Book and was also mentioned as early as AD 753. In 1086 108 people were recorded on the manor of Hayes, one of whom was a priest and three were knights. The land was owned by the then Archbishop of Canterbury, most of it being arable and pasture with large areas of wood. The Archbishop of Canterbury owned a house in Hayes at that time which was known as the 'House of Anselm', where meetings of bishops were held.

The parish church of St Mary in Hayes is a flint rubble building and has much of interest. The font dates from about 1200 and all the roofs are original, despite the church having been restored in 1873. There are also medieval wall paintings of St Christopher.

Manor Lodge which stood in Freeman's Lane was built in the first half of the 17th century and was originally the vicarage. It was sold by the rector in about 1865 and renamed Manor Lodge. During the two World Wars the house was used as the company headquarters of a Local Home Guard battalion, but it fell derelict after the war and was demolished.

Hayes Court was another historic house which is now gone. Adjoining St Mary's churchyard, it had close connections with the manor of Hayes. It was demolished about 1968 and the site is now a car park!

The Manor House in Church Road dates from the 17th century but traces of a moat and discoveries of pottery indicate that a medieval house may have occupied the site. The house was extensively altered in about 1862, and was then occupied by the rector and renamed Rectory Manor House. The house was used as a remand home for boys in the 1930s, when the greater part of the east end was destroyed by fire. The remaining part of the house today is the centre of a new small housing estate. Famous visitors to the manor of Hayes were Queen Elizabeth I and Queen Anne. The Wesley brothers also visited Hayes.

Hayes Park was owned by Robert Willis Blencowe at the time of Hayes Enclosure in 1814 and by 1845 was the seat of Colonel James Grant. He does not appear to have lived there very long, since the 1851 census shows that by then it was a private lunatic asylum, under the supervision of William Conolley, MRCS. There were ten patients described as 'gentlemen' and one peer – Francis Stewart, 11th Earl of Moray. The house remained an asylum and later a nursing home until it was purchased, together with the surrounding parkland by H. J. Heinz Co Ltd, who demolished it during the 1960s in order to build a food research centre.

The Thomas Triplett Charity was founded by a deed in

1668 securing property in Suffolk to pay among other charitable donations £15 a year for apprenticing the poor children of Hayes.

In the early 19th century only four inns were to be found in Hayes, the Waggon and Horses, White Hart, Angel and Adam and Eve. Thereafter public houses proliferated and by 1864 there were at least 18.

Although the number of commercial premises increased during the later 19th century the appearance of the parish altered little before 1900. A few factories in Dawley Road and a small terrace of houses along North Hyde Road (formerly known as Ford Lane) were built.

The Great Western Railway Station at Hayes and Harlington was opened in 1864. Transport facilities improved and between 1901 and 1903 the London United Tramways Co extended its line from Southall to Uxbridge along the main road. Brickmaking was the first industry to appear in Hayes, and its development probably resulted from the opening of the Grand Junction Canal in 1796.

Sixty years ago there were approximately ten or twelve farms in Hayes including quite a few dairy farms. Watercress used to be grown in fresh water springs near the Splash in North Hyde Road, and there were several springs and ponds in the district. Various cottages were built in the area.

Ploughing matches were an annual feature at many farms, and many workers would get ten shillings and a certificate for a year's loyal service, which they would frame and hang on the wall of their parlours.

The first electric light in Hayes was installed at the Beck engineering works in the High Road, on a signboard outside the main entrance and the local people called it the 'Beacon'. Small local shops included Bridge Heath's dining rooms and hardware shop, the post office on the corner of Silverdale Road, Maxwell's newsagent's and barber's, Platt's Stores in Clayton Road, Rose's cycle shop and Mrs Young's in Austin Road, where children used to go with a basin to buy a penny worth of jam, treacle or pickles, which were kept in big storage jars under the counter and ladled out.

The Hebrew Industrial School stood in the Uxbridge Road on the corner of Coldharbour Lane. It was opened in 1901 as an industrial school for delinquent Jewish boys. It was among the first establishments of its kind to train boys for skilled occupation after release, and instruction was given in woodwork and metalwork, together with school lessons and physical training. Lord Rothschild donated £6,000 towards the cost of the school, and the bulk of the rest of the money came from the Jewish community. The school was eventually renamed St Christopher's. Following a new concept in the care of young persons it was demolished and replaced by the St Christopher's Community House on a nearby site – the first of its kind in the country.

Two factories now sprang up in Hayes, one in Blythe Road in 1911 for Goss Printing Press Ltd. In the First World War this was used for the manufacture of cars and lorries by the McCurdy Lorry Manufacturing Co Ltd. This company had a slogan 'Thought out first – not found out afterwards'! The site now belongs to the EMI Group (now one of the largest employers in Hayes) but the building still has traces of the McCurdy title high up on the wall on the east side.

The National Filling Factory No 7 was one of a number built in 1915 at the instigation of Lloyd George, Minister of Munitions to augment supplies of shells for the Army. It occupied a large site south of the railway almost down to where the M4 motorway at Cranford is now. The sheds were widely spaced and connected by wooden walkways to avoid the risk of explosion. Twelve thousand people, most of them women, were employed there and Hayes became a boom town. On the 23rd October 1917 a serious accident occurred when many women workers were killed or injured.

There was an increasing demand for cottages and houses as several large factories were built during the 1920s and

1930s. The industrial concentration round Botwell greatly expanded with the appearance of such firms as Nestle's, Kraft, and Smith's Potato Crisps. By 1944 Hayes was considered to be over-industrialised and the labour saturation point had been passed. Many houses were built in the 1930s and building continued after the Second World War.

In 1950 a factory in Hayes was acquired by the Public Record Office as an intermediate depository where departmental records could be sorted before destruction or transfer for preservation in the Public Records Office itself.

St Anselm's, a mission church, was re-built in 1928 when it formed the new parish church for Botwell.

A cinema was opened in Botwell in 1926 (on the now Woolworth site) and two others were being built in Uxbridge Road in 1938. These have now been closed and there is now a Bingo hall on one site in Uxbridge Road. Other recreational facilities now in Hayes are the local Hayes Football Club, founded in 1909, the Working Men's Club in Pump Lane and pride of place goes to the Beck Theatre situated in Grange Road near to the Botanical Gardens and the Hayes Cricket Club. There is also the Hesa Arts Society.

Hayes also has a cottage hospital which it has fought to retain, a fire station, and Hayes Divisional Police Station on the Uxbridge Road.

Hillingdon 🦢

The village lies on the old London to Oxford road about one and a half miles to the south-east of the ancient market town of Uxbridge. The earliest spelling of the name is 'Hillendone'.

The parish church of St John the Baptist stands on high ground and is the focal point of the village. The chancel arch dates back to circa 1260 whilst the nave and aisles are mid

The Church of St John the Baptist, Hillingdon

14th century. The west tower was rebuilt in 1629 and the staircase is original and has pilaster balusters. The chancel and transepts were added by Gilbert Scott in 1848. There are two fine monuments in the chancel and an outstanding memorial brass of 1509 depicts John L'Estrange and his wife Jacquette Woodville. John Rich, the 18th century actor-manager, lies buried in the churchyard.

Nearby is the Red Lion inn where King Charles I stopped on 27th April 1646 when on his way from Oxford to join his allies in the North. Almost next door stands The Cottage, now an hotel, a 16th century timber framed building that earlier this century was the home of Christopher Stone, an early radio personality and co-founder of *The Gramophone* magazine.

Across the main road opposite the church is The Cedar House, an Elizabethan mansion which takes its name from one of the first cedars ever to be planted in this country. This was in 1683 when the owner was botanist Samuel Reynardson. The building is now the headquarters of a firm of civil engineers.

In Royal Lane, to the south of the church, is Bishopshalt, a Victorian mansion built on the site of the original manor house of Hillingdon. For nearly six centuries the site belonged to the Bishops of Worcester who halted there on their way to and from London. Bishopshalt, enlarged in the 1920s, is now a comprehensive school.

Hillingdon Fair, held annually in mid-May, dates from the founding of a chantry in 1372. Legend has it that a curse put on the fair many years ago ensures that rain always spoils the event!

The arrival of electric trams in 1904 heralded many changes although for a few years after the Second World War Farmer Bunce was still leading his cows through the village to be milked. In 1935 Hillingdon Hill became a dual carriageway and the trams gave way to trolley buses.

One of the notable people of the area was the Hon. Charles T. Mills who was elected to Parliament in 1910. Unfortunately, he was killed in France in 1915 but was replaced as Member of Parliament by his brother, the Hon. A. R. Mills. Their mother, the Dowager Lady Hillingdon, unveiled the war memorial which stood near St Andrew's church, Uxbridge, until it was moved in the 1970s to the old burial ground in Uxbridge. Other well-known names of Hillingdon village were Mitchell (saddler) and Buttrum (builder).

Many people still remember the lovely old trees which stood in the village. One, an elm, was ravaged by Dutch Elm disease and there was an old oak tree near the Red Lion inn which was severely lopped in the 1920s. This onslaught led to a villager displaying a placard on which was the single word 'Ichabod', which means 'the glory has departed'. How true this is of many of our lovely old buildings, grounds and gardens.

Today the village lies at the geographical centre of the London Borough of Hillingdon, four miles to the north of Heathrow airport and within easy reach of the M4, M25 and M40 motorways. Yet, amazingly, Hillingdon village, now a conservation area, still retains something of the atmosphere of the past centuries.

Ickenham ❧

The name Ickenham derived from the 'ham', meaning village, of Ticca, an Anglo-Saxon leader. References to the village are in the Domesday Book.

Ickenham was included in the Hundred of Elthorne and was originally made up mainly of farmers. Each farmer's land was divided up into strips, each estimated to take him a day to work, the main crops being wheat, barley and oats.

The Almshouses at Ickenham

The church was built in the 14th century and enlarged in the 16th century. Amongst its monuments is one to the baby son of Sir Robert Clayton, dated 1665, who died within a few hours of his birth. The little figure carved in marble, wrapped in swaddling clothes, is very touching. St Giles' first rector was John Payne, 1335–1353, and since then 45 rectors are recorded to the present day.

The Congregational church was opened in 1835, but with an increasing attendance a larger building was needed and a hundred years later in 1936 a new church was opened and dedicated. The size of the community in Ickenham continued to grow, but was still only 443 in 1921, with an increase to 1,741 in 1931.

The first school in Ickenham began around 1819 with some 50 children in attendance. They were not full time, having to help on the farm, collect wood etc. The school was maintained by the more well off families and teaching was mainly carried out by older children who themselves had only rudimentary knowledge. By 1866 a school building was erected and by 1873 it had a schoolmistress and 37 pupils. There are now two junior and two senior schools in Ickenham, though children do attend from other areas.

Leisure time for the pupils of 1873 was very short. Even the picking of blackberries or the gathering of acorns was done for money, and it would prevent them from attending school, as did birdscaring and beating for local shoots. The highlights of their lives must have been the surrounding district's annual fairs, as well as Ickenham's own, which sadly lost its right to hold one in 1936. No one came to erect a stall in that year, hence the 'right' had gone. Occasions which did officially excuse the children from school were mostly sad times when they would attend the funeral of a member of their family, a classmate or school official, for epidemics of scarlet fever, chicken pox etc, were still taking their toll.

After the First World War it was decided that funds should be raised to build a Memorial Hall. Here probably was the first recreational establishment in Ickenham. For a shilling a share funds were raised to purchase the land and build Ickenham's village hall, which was opened in January 1927. The hall is in constant use and Ickenham is a thriving active community. Every alternate year a week long Festival is held during June, and for eight days the village of Ickenham is a place of fun, laughter and gaiety.

In this modern day the 'village' of Ickenham is hardly a village in the true sense with its population of around 12,000 people. However its inhabitants still enjoy the village atmosphere, and there is a feeling of welcome to the visitor today just as Samuel Pepys discovered so long ago when visiting Swakeleys manor house.

Swakeleys has for hundreds of years been the 'seat' of Ickenham. The earliest record of it is in 1326 when Swakeleys was owned by Robert Swalclyve. The present house was built between 1629 and 1638 by Sir Edmund Wright, later

Lord Mayor of London. The rainwater heads at the house are all dated 1638.

Pepys came to Swakeleys on 7th September 1665 to visit Sir Robert Vyner. He thought it 'a very pleasant place', although 'not very modern in the garden nor house'. 'The window cases, door cases and chimneys of all the house are marble. He showed me a black boy that he had, that died of a consumption, and being dead, he caused him to be dried in an oven, and lies there entire in a box.' On which revolting note, Pepys went in to dinner!

Swakeleys now has a new life. The building was saved by a group of local people who risked all, then managed to find a company prepared to restore the building to its former glory. It now stands proudly in its lovely grounds, having been re-opened by Prince Philip and is used as offices. The house is open to the public four days a year and the grounds to the Festival Committee.

Isleworth 🪴

The ancient settlement of Isleworth was mentioned in the Domesday Book as Gistelesworde. There is a tradition that Caesar crossed the river Thames here, and King Canute and the Danes also crossed the river in AD 1016. Later Isleworth was the scene of the Battle of Brentford, fought between the Roundheads and the Cavaliers, during the Civil War.

The old town of Isleworth was spread along the river and back to Old Isleworth Square, much of the river frontage being taken up by Syon House, the home of the Duke of Northumberland. Syon monastery was founded by Henry V in 1415 and moved to the site of the present house in 1431. The regime was a strict one and silence was enforced. Sign language was therefore necessary at times and the chronicles

Syon House at Isleworth

record useful tips. To ask for mustard at a meal, for instance, 'Hold thy nose in the uppere part of the right fist and rubbe it'!

After the Dissolution of the Monasteries, Syon passed to the Duke of Somerset and then, after the Duke's execution, to John Dudley, Earl of Northumberland. History has been made at Syon over the centuries. Catherine Howard, Henry VIII's fifth wife, was imprisoned there and left the house only to go to her death in the Tower. Later Henry's body lay at Syon on its way from Westminster to Windsor. In 1553 Lady Jane Grey was proclaimed Queen at Syon.

Syon House today owes its general appearance to mid 16th century building, but in 1761 Robert Adam was commissioned to carry out extensive alterations.

Isleworth parish church of All Saints, which stands by the river, is on the site of one built in Saxon times. The present church is mainly modern, having been rebuilt after the Second World War and re-dedicated in 1970. The tower and the outer shell were all that remained of the old building after a fire in 1943, started by some local boys.

Isleworth once boasted many fine houses but very few are left now. Nazareth House and Gumley House are both convents. Gumley House was built in the 17th century and in the reign of Queen Anne was occupied by a rich glass manufacturer called Gumley. His beautiful daughter married William Pulteney, later Earl of Bath, and they lived at the house after Gumley's death. The house became a fashionable centre and the Earl's wife is described, very unflatteringly, in Pope's *The Looking Glass*.

Isleworth's background consisted for centuries of agriculture and river trade. The market gardens and fruit farms are gone now, one of the last being at Ivybridge. In 1635 'The Isleworth Survey' noted that the 'ayre of Istelworth is wonderful, temperate and healthful'! The wharves of old Isleworth were busy with cranes, and timber and coal were transported from Lion Wharf until recent years. 1987 saw the demolition of the old river buildings and a whole new complex of shops, offices and flats have been built.

Many large companies have office blocks here now. There is also a large teaching hospital, the West Middlesex, and a sewage works in Mogden Lane. In the grounds of Syon House there is a large garden centre, with the added attraction of a butterfly house.

Luckily, the charming houses in Church Street have been preserved, and although the new buildings have their critics, on the whole most people think they sit very comfortably alongside their Georgian neighbours.

Iver 🦢

Though just over the official boundary line, Iver is included here as its WI belongs to the Middlesex Federation. Iver's history goes back into the mists of time. It was mentioned in a chronicle of AD 893 and in the Domesday Book.

The church dates back to Saxon times, though it is now mainly Norman with later additions. It stands at the foot of the High Street, guarding the main entrance from Uxbridge.

Many famous people are buried in the churchyard including a royal prince – Admiral Lord Gambier. The first garden pansies were developed from the wild by the Prince's gardener, Thompson, in 1815.

The churchyard and surroundings are still a sanctuary for the hard pressed local wild flora. In a survey, the Iver & District Countryside Association found 97 species of flowers, ferns and mosses (some of them rare), 20 trees and 14 grasses.

The sister of Cecil Rhodes, founder of Rhodesia (now Zimbabwe), lived in Iver Lodge, Cecil Road being named after him.

There is still in existence the 'posse commetatus' of 1798, a record of the 334 village men 'called up' for the Napoleonic Wars.

In the 1800s the Swan and the Bull pubs were staging posts for coaches from Windsor and Burnham to Uxbridge and London. The mail coaches called twice a day. At the turn of the century, 'Shaker' Thether Butler ran a passenger horse brake to Uxbridge. The speed limit in the village was 10 mph!

Johnny Hall, to celebrate the relief of Mafeking in the Boer War, rolled a flaming barrel of tar down the High Street. He was a local character, who drove around in a pony and trap, always carrying his Bible. He often gave lifts to local lads, but was not above dumping them into the river ford!

There are strong royal connections in Iver. It was the home of the Duke of Kent and Princess Marina, who lived in the house called Coppins, left them by Princess Victoria, youngest daughter of Queen Victoria. Their children grew up here, and later it became the home of the present Duke of Kent until, a sad sign of our times, they were advised to leave because it could not be made sufficiently secure. Princess Alexandra maintains an interest in the village, opening the new village hall that the community had planned and raised money for over a long period of time.

About 1912, Guste Hemul, who flew the mail from Hendon to Windsor, caused great excitement when he landed his small plane at Richings Park.

During the Second World War some government departments along with London children were evacuated to Iver. During this time the women of the village coped with such delicacies as carrot cake and chocolate pudding using stale bread, milk, cocoa and syrup. Later came instructions on how to serve bully beef to demobbed soldiers! Just after the war a local magistrate banned a fish and chip van because it might make the hay smell!

The face of Iver has changed many times. It had long been an agricultural centre with many small farms or holdings on common land. The Enclosure Act of 1801 divided the land amongst new landlords, making fewer and larger estates.

The 1851 census showed that the parish of Iver extended to Oak End at Gerrards Cross, and the main occupations for men were agriculture and brickmaking. It was a familiar sight at the turn of the century to see women and children taking their menfolk's dinner out to the brickfields tied up in a red and white cloth, the tea in tin cans. The brickfields are long gone but some farms still remain.

The Slough arm of the Grand Junction Canal was built

around 1880 to carry bricks and gravel to London. The barges returned full of refuse from West London for dumping into the gravel pits.

The mansion at Richings Park surrounded by open fields is no more. The news of the coming of the railway prompted the building of Richings Park housing estate in 1920. Industry began moving into the area and now there is the Ridgeway industrial estate, housing such international names as Faberge and Bison. Pinewood Studios, of James Bond fame, is at Iver Heath.

The railway opened in 1924 enabling London business men to live in Iver and commute. The rate of change was relatively slow, the small friendly village grew into a large friendly village, still keeping its sense of community as more people moved in.

Many pop and film stars moved into the surrounding area, but gradually the pace quickened and now the village is under attack from many quarters as building increases. Evreham, the small local comprehensive school is to close and so is the small cottage hospital, paid for by local subscription and where local GP's look after their own patients.

A service station with an enormous carpark is to be built at Iver railway station, with a linking train service to Heathrow. Hillingdon Greater London Borough is laying claim to all land up to the newly built M25, thereby annexing land and houses now part of Iver. This large parish, 15 miles from London will have London on its doorstep, the M25 running only yards from Iver church.

Kenton

Kenton: 'A dream little hamlet set in a sea of emerald with a few cottages, a couple of farmhouses and a little inn.'

One may be forgiven for failing to recognise Kenton in this description written at the end of the 19th century. Even after

St. Mary the Virgin
Kenton

the First World War this hamlet, that lies to the east of Harrow, still had a population barely exceeding 250. From the mid 1920s however, in common with its neighbouring hamlets and villages, Kenton was transformed into an extensive suburban area.

Kenton has few buildings of distinction apart from the parish church of St Mary the Virgin (1936). The modern Gothic tower of yellow brick with stone dressing is a major feature of the district. The Roman Catholic church of All Saints further east is a smaller, later and perhaps more adventurous edifice with a campanile.

The two public houses along the main Kenton Road stand on sites of earlier refreshment houses. The present Travellers Rest, by the railway bridge, was reputed to be the largest public house in Middlesex when it was erected in 1933, while the present Plough replaced in 1926 an inn that is believed to have held a licence since the first half of the 18th century.

Near to the Plough but concealed by a copse from the road, is Kenton Grange. Built in the 19th century, it was the most impressive habitation of the old hamlet. It stood in 27 acres and contained lakes, pastureland, orchards, stables and later an extensive miniature railway complex. The Grange had various owners but the American tobacco tycoon, Albert J. Jeffress was probably the most colourful. The house remained in the Jeffress family until it was sold in 1951 to become a home for the elderly. The grounds now form part of an attractive park.

Despite Kenton's bland 20th century appearance, its history goes back, as its name suggests, to Saxon times: Kentun, 'the farm of the sons of Coena'.

On Kenton's eastern boundary with Kingsbury, the Saxons assembled in a wedge-shaped field or 'Gore'. Here the Hundred Court adjudicated and open air courts for the Hundred of Gore were held. The Metropolitan Police No. 7

Area HQ (NW) now stands upon the site but inscribed in stone one may read: 'This building stands on the site of the Moot (meeting place) of the Hundred of Gore'.

The first written record relating to Kenton goes back to AD 767 when Offa, King of the Mercians, exchanged lands with Stidberht, 'holy man and abbot'. Thus virtually all the land we know today as Kenton became the property of the Church and remained so until the Reformation.

Often must those early archbishops like Lanfranc, Anselm and Becket have cast their eyes across Kenton's fields and woodland as they travelled from Westminster to their manor at Harrow. Through these same pastures in the 16th century walked John Lyon, founder of Harrow School, as he journeyed each Sunday from his nearby farm at Preston to worship at the parish church on Harrow Hill. About the same time, but with stealthier steps, came the Jesuit priests and other Catholic fugitives escaping from their Protestant pursuers. They were seeking the sanctuary of the farmhouse of the Bellamy family that stood alongside Kenton Brook at Uxendon. Knowing only too well the dreadful consequences of sheltering Catholics, the Bellamy's courage did not waver. One by one the family paid the ultimate penalty for their unfaltering faith.

Few of today's frustrated motorists driving along the congested Kenton Road are aware that the highway was formerly known as Tyburn Lane, so called because it terminated at Tyburn Tree. Another sinister reminder of a cruel past.

Laleham on Thames ✒

The name Laleham comes from the Anglo-Saxon 'laela' meaning twig or withy and 'hamm', meaning a water meadow. This village in 'a river meadow where withies abound' is mentioned in 10th century documents. Laleham is now part of the Borough of Spelthorne.

The river Thames is a specific feature of the village and is rather picturesque, attracting many people to camp and spend days by the river, instead of joining the rush to the sea.

The lord of the manor is Lord Lucan, the 7th Earl, who disappeared under mysterious circumstances in 1974, but who has not been declared legally dead. The Lucan family no longer live in the village.

In 1819 Dr Thomas Arnold, who became the well known headmaster of Rugby school, and his brother-in-law John Buckland, who founded the English prep school system, moved into the village. Six of the Arnold children, including the poet Matthew, were born in Laleham. Matthew Arnold and his three sons are buried in Laleham churchyard.

It was Thomas Arnold and John Buckland who began education in the village. Arnold's house was on a site now covered by the vicarage, the Glebe House and part of the present school, and he prepared boys there for university entrance. Buckland began a small school for the preparation of boys for boarding school.

Laleham National School was opened in 1865, built by the 3rd Earl Lucan. The Lucan family showed a great deal of interest in the progress of the school and their coat of arms is on the south wall of the original building.

There are two churches in Laleham. Laleham Methodist church is on the Royal Estate (so called because all the roads have royal names), a reasonably modern church built since the Second World War. All Saints church stands in the centre of the village and is believed to stand on the site of a small Roman temple. Although from the outside it appears to be 19th century, inside it has one of only two Norman arcades in the county.

Many famous people have lived in Laleham, apart from the Arnolds, including Bob Hope, Gertrude Lawrence and

Richard Tauber. Edward VII when he was Prince of Wales, was a regular visitor to the Three Horseshoes public house when he stayed with the Lucan family at Laleham House. Another famous patron was Sir Arthur Sullivan (of Gilbert and Sullivan).

Those who live in Laleham still think of it as a village, but as it sits on one of the richest gravel seams in the county its peace has suffered from the number of gravel pits surrounding it.

Lampton 🌿

Lampton years ago was a tiny village, with just Lampton Hall, a few cottages and a couple of inns, the White Horse and the Black Horse. The latter inn was known to have been in existence by 1759 and was rebuilt in 1926. Lampton Lane (now Road) from Heston to Hounslow was gated on both the Heston side and the Lampton side, somewhere near to the junction of the Great West Road crossing of today, to prevent the straying of animals. The lane itself was narrow, with elm trees growing in the hedgerows. It has been widened at least twice over the years.

There was a pond in the grounds of the Highlands, a large house past the Black Horse towards Hounslow, now demolished. Another pond was near Sunnycroft Road, and a third where Hounslow Central Station is. This pond was in the grounds of the old Hounslow manor house, fed by the stream which ran along the line now used by the railway, under the Leets and the Broadway to St John's Road, and eventually into the Thames. This stream, one of the 'drains to the heath', was a fair size and drained the land south of Heston. In Lampton Lane there was a 'splash', locally called a 'splosh', used by vehicles, though for those on foot there was a bridge known as Bason Bridge.

There was a pathway from Heston to Isleworth known as the 'Hedges'. Parts remain today, but not all the way to Isleworth. As Lampton Road developed many large houses were built by the prosperous members of the Hounslow community but not many of these remain now. The new Civic Centre for the London Borough of Hounslow has been built in the grounds of two of these, while the houses themselves form part of the administration offices. The Elms farm, once known as 'Old Sally Roger's Farm', opposite The Lawn and at the end of the last century lived in by Mr Alfred Platt, founder of Platt's Stores, was demolished in the early part of this century to make way for Elmsworth Avenue, Avonwick Road, and Sunnycroft Road.

After the First World War the Great West Road was constructed and opened by King George V in 1925. From this date to the outbreak of the Second World War, much building and development took place. The new factories on the Great West Road from Syon Lane to Chiswick became quite a showpiece, especially after dark with the neon signs. The desirable residences built on the Great West Road were and remain today much sought after.

Two parades of shops appeared at the Lampton junction, one on each side of the Great West Road, and land which had been part of the grounds of Lampton Hall was developed. The Hall at this time was occupied by Major Bisgood. In the past it is known that Charles Dickens used to visit the Hall when he lived at St Margarets, and he continued to come to see his friends after he had moved to Petersham. In the 1940s it was acquired by Glyn Mills Bank and they have built another office block in the grounds.

Further along the Great West Road, the Ace of Spades Road House was built in the 1930s, catering for the ever increasing number of motorists. The petrol station, restaurant, cocktail bar and open air swimming pool soon became very popular, and enjoyed quite a 'racy' reputation.

92

The outbreak of the Second World War saw its closure, only to open briefly after the war before a new development.

On the land between the Ace of Spades and the footpath known as the 'Hedges' it was planned to build a school, but this was postponed until after the war. This was a blessing as a doodle bug dropped there in 1944! However this land was put to good use growing vegetables, and Italian POW's were brought in by coaches to tend the land.

Littleton 🌿

In the 1930s, a few years after the Queen Mary reservoir had flooded the neighbouring hamlet of Astlam, Littleton was still a little village, one of the smallest Middlesex parishes. Grouped about the village green, it had never had a pub or shop, but there were some attractive old houses, a blacksmith and a church and vicarage.

The brick church of St Mary Magdalene is of Norman origin, the nave and chancel dating from the 13th century. The choir stalls and chancel wall panelling were formerly in Winchester Cathedral.

Littleton Park was owned by Sir Guy de Bryen in 1350, the estate apparently having been given as a reward to Sir Guy for his services as Standard Bearer to Edward III in 1347 when Calais was taken. In the 17th century Sir Christopher Wren is thought to have been involved in the building of the house, but the present house dates from the rebuilding after a fire in 1874. The oak ceiling of the main hall came from the old House of Commons and there are a great number of items of interest in the house as a whole. It is said that the ghost of Lady Caroline Wood walks in the house, wearing a red dress. She had a tragic, but romantic, demise, having thrown herself down a stairwell because her lover had jilted her.

Littleton Park is, of course, better known as the home of Shepperton film studios. In the 1930s the studios were called 'Sound City'!

Longford ✑

Longford is a small village on the old Bath Road, very close to the north-west corner of Heathrow airport.

There are a few buildings dating from the 17th and 18th centuries and a famous pub called The Peggy Bedford, originally known as The King's Head. Peggy Bedford was the landlord's wife there in the 19th century and died in 1859. The old pub burned down in the late 19th century and was rebuilt in the 1930s as The Peggy Bedford.

The Longford river was diverted from the Colne river in Longford by Charles I, to improve the water supply to Hampton Court, and it was formerly known as the Hampton Court Cut. In the late 1940s the Longford river together with the Duke of Northumberland's river (another artificial river) was diverted southwards to form a single channel, and allow for the extensive development of Heathrow airport. This man-made river still supplies the ornamental ponds and fountains at Hampton Court.

Northolt ✑

Northolt was once 'a sleepy little hollow' when it consisted of farms, a pub, a forge, a general shop with post lady, one tin chapel and the church. The settlement is over a thousand years old and it did not begin to grow until the 1930s.

St Mary's church dates back to the 13th century and stands on a hill beyond the still lovely village green with the small brook running through it.

The earliest burial recorded in Northolt was of a Henry Rowdell on 10th April 1452. There is a brass plate covering his grave in the south aisle of the church. He was the owner of an estate now covered by lands known as Catherine Mead and Smith Farm.

Until 1908 the village school was also up on the hill, having only two classrooms. It became the parish hall, and in the mid 1930s was renamed the Memorial Hall in memory of Charles Baker, a local benefactor.

Where the Load of Hay, a renowned public house/restaurant stands today was the site of the parish workhouse in 1806. The inmates were allowed to work on local farms and could earn up to 1/6d per week. Their laid down diet consisted of, for breakfast, milk pottage, broth or water gruel. Dinner and supper alternated between bread, butter and 4 oz cheese and 'wholesome butcher's meat'. Three pints of beer per person per day was allowed if required.

Northolt was mainly a farming area with six or seven farms, mostly pig breeding and hay producing. When the Grand Junction Canal was cut through Northolt, running from Paddington to the Midlands, it was a great help to the farmers, since hay could be sent by barge instead of by waggonette on the then very rough country lanes to London.

Until the early 1920s sheep grazed on the village green. A pump served the villagers on the green until the late 1920s. In the year 1910 the Parish Council debated and resolved that 'No geese be allowed on the village green between 25th March and 29th September'. On 5th July 1911 a notice was served on a Mrs Reed, who did not heed the resolution. It is interesting to note that the 'geese' won the day!

In early years the Royal Buck Hounds used to meet at Northolt two or three times a year on the village green. The stag hounds assembled on a field near the present Target public house and they would hunt on Lord Hillingdon's land. In 1914 he sold some of his land in Ruislip parish and it became Northolt airport.

Northolt's rural atmosphere has survived despite the surrounding inter-war suburban development. The green is dominated by the Crown public house, which together with a few cottages, shops and other buildings represents the last remnants of the former country village of Northolt. Policies will be aimed at preserving the rural qualities and the intimate charm of this picturesque area.

Northwood 🌿

Today, Northwood is a thriving dormitory for London. Daily the early morning trains on the Metropolitan line fill up with commuters bound for the City and in the evening they are delivered back again. Within easy reach of London and also of the countryside, well served by excellent schools, both public and private, and a number of splendid golf courses, Northwood is indeed ideal commuter-land. But it was not until the middle of the 19th century that Northwood took on an identity of its own, and the opening of the railway station in 1887 was the chief milestone on the road to the present day.

Up until that time Northwood was a hamlet in the parish of Ruislip. In fact Northwood was the name of a house in the hamlet, there was no village of that name. The earliest reference is to be found in 13th century records relating to the famous Abbey of Bec where a 'Norwode' would seem to refer to a grange in the manor of Ruislip. During Henry IV's reign all French abbeys were seized and so the Bec lands became Crown property until they were leased to Kings College, Cambridge. Although the College has disposed of all its land it still remains the titular lord of the manor.

Today a house of 15th century origin called The Grange stands on or near the site of the Abbey of Bec's granges. It is interesting to read in the letters of the daughters of a one-time owner Dr Nash, of appearances of a ghostly monk and the sound of monastic footsteps! Today the Grange is council property and is used by local organisations for meetings.

It is interesting to note that Northwood's only old inn is the Gate at Kewferry Hill. It derives its name from a toll gate which was in use up to about 1875. The exact age of the inn is not known but it was probably built between 1600 and 1650.

The opening of Northwood railway station began the transformation to the Northwood of today and its physical lay-out and social structure owes much to one Frank Carew, a great grandson of one of Lord Nelson's captains. He stipulated the prices of the houses to be built on the land which he had sold to the builders and his long list of Christian names together with his surname were used to name some of the new roads – Murray, Maxwell, Hallowell, Carew. To these were added those of his wife Edith Chester, and his sons Roy and Reginald. He lived in Eastbury House at the time, but the house has changed hands many times since then, and during the last war became the headquarters of RAF Coastal Command, which in turn has become part of the greatly enlarged NATO Headquarters.

Another building which played its part in war but this time the First World War was St John's church, Hallowell Road, which was used as a VAD hospital.

There is so much history behind this pleasant residential area, but those who have lived here for 50 years or more have watched the demise of the friendly corner shop and the advent of the inevitable supermarket.

Norwood Green 🪶

Norwood Green is an ancient village still centred on its common green in spite of the encroachment of suburbia and the efforts of developers.

The church of St Mary the Virgin is one of the village's proudest possessions, rebuilt during the reign of Henry VI by Archbishop Henry Chichele. It boasts an interesting total immersion font, one of the finest in the country and a famous pipe organ built by Bevington, which attracts organists from many places.

Directly opposite the church is a public house, The Plough is built of oak beams held together with dowelling, many of which can now be seen in the British Museum. Also in the Museum are the touch marks of the masons who worked on the rebuilding of the church. These were found struck into a beam in the Plough during restoration work – evidently graffiti is not a new pastime!

The village has an association with the famous engineer and architect Isambard Kingdom Brunel, who designed one of the most interesting bridges in England. Known as 'Three Bridges', it is at the eastern end of the parish and carries a railway, a canal and a road one above the other all at one point and is therefore probably the only place where you could drop something overboard from a boat and have it land on a train!

This is still very much a village community, the focus of which has only moved a matter of yards in several hundred years from the village pump which still stands on the green in front of the Wolf pub to the local sub post office, which is now the exchange of information point for the village. The Wolf was involved until recently in an old local custom, the annual 'Wolf and Lamb' cricket match that was played on the green for the honour of holding and displaying a giant

Norwood Hall, Norwood Green

cricket bat for the year. The Lamb public house faces the Wolf across the Norwood Road. The bat can still be seen on the front of the last winner.

The Lamb stands on the bank of the Grand Junction Canal beside another interesting bridge. This was the first ferro-concrete bridge to be built and the local authorities were far from convinced about its safety. They therefore had eight heavily laden Foden steam lorries driven over the bridge at speed to test it before opening it to public use. The first one might have gone over at even greater speed if he had been told it might not hold him!

The Grand Union Canal has played an important part in the history of the area and for many years this was the site of the Barge School where the children of the bargees could learn to read and write. There is also in the parish a Free

School established in 1767 by Elisha Biscoe for the education of 34 boys and six girls of poor families. His will stated that,

> 'girls are to be taught reading, writing and plain work, knitting and house business in order to make them good servants'.

Village Day, held in July, is the high point of the year. It originated as a hiring fair for the local workers and farmers. Now all local groups support it. Everyone attends and there are produce stalls, local handicrafts, competitions and a large flower show that always attracts beautiful exhibits.

Osterley ꙮ

There is little of the distant past to be found in Osterley, except for its famous house and gardens. St Mary's church was only built in 1856 and much of the building is of the late 19th and 20th centuries. Expansion really began when the new Great West Road opened in the 1920s and the railway station was built in 1934 – villas, shops and factories soon followed.

The manor is known to have belonged to John of Osterlee in the time of Edward I. After various owners it came into the possession of Sir Thomas Gresham, founder of the Royal Exchange, who built himself a mansion in 1577. He also enclosed part of Hounslow Heath for his park, which proved very unpopular with the villagers because it affected their common rights. Compensation had to be paid!

Sir Thomas entertained Queen Elizabeth I in his new house in 1578. He also became the first person to introduce oranges into England. The splendour of Osterley faded after his death and the estate passed through many hands until it was bought by the banker, Sir Francis Child, in 1711. The house

100

and grounds were transformed between 1761 and 1780 by Robert Adam for the Child family.

The estate came into the hands of the 5th Earl of Jersey by marriage in 1802 and in 1949 the 9th Earl presented the house and estate to the National Trust. The Victoria and Albert Museum are custodians of the 18th century furniture. A fine outside staircase designed by Robert Adam is still in existence, as is the Doric temple.

When the Earl gave the park to the nation it comprised some 650 acres and it became one of the great open spaces of Greater London. However in 1960 it was torn apart by the construction of the M4 motorway and today the National Trust owns all that is left, a mere 140 acres. The Department of the Environment, through the Royal Parks Department, aims to restore the gardens to their former glory.

Perivale 🎐

Perivale appears in the Domesday Book as 'Greneford Parva' or 'Little Greenford'. Before the Norman invasion, the woodlands and 300 acres of cultivated land which made up the parish were held by a vassal of the Saxon Ansgar, Master of the Stud to Edward the Confessor, but from 1086 the 50 or so inhabitants found themselves under a new lord of the manor, Geoffrey de Mandeville, one of the first great feudal barons created by William the Conqueror for services in battle.

Perivale changed little during the next few centuries except in name, 'Cornhill', 'Parevale' and 'Peryvale' are just some of the variations used in old records. Their origins probably come from the abundance of good wheat which covered the fertile farmlands of the Brent valley and the slopes of Horsenden Hill during the Middle Ages. Other references suggest that the wine or 'perry' made from the numerous pear trees in the orchards could also have been responsible. Henry Myllet declared himself 'Lord of the Toune' in 1573 and built the moated manor house west of the church – Perivale Park now covers this site. This was a prosperous time for Perivale.

By 1801, when the Paddington arm of the Grand Junction Canal pushed its way through Perivale there were only 28 people living on the five large hay farms which provided much of the hay for London's horses.

Agriculture was still the main occupation and there were less than 24 houses in the area when the Great Western Railway passed through Perivale and Greenford at the beginning of the 20th century. With the building of the Western Avenue during the 1920s fields and farmlands gradually gave way to factories and housing estates.

The church of St Mary the Virgin has stood close to the river Brent since 1185. Additions and alterations were made to the original church in the 15th and 18th centuries. In 1976 St Mary's was declared redundant (although it remains consecrated) and was leased to the Friends of St Mary's Trust.

A delightful legend surrounds Horsenden Hill. The story concerns a mythical Saxon chief called Horsa whose wife's nightly revels with elfin folk in the vale below their hillside residence earned it the name of 'Fairyvale' or Perivale. Their only child, Ealine, was a beautiful girl who, after learning everything her mother could teach her, became something of a child prodigy. She fell in love and married Bren, the handsome chief of a powerful tribe on the banks of the Thames. But far from living happily ever after Ealine soon discovered that her new husband preferred carousing with the local lads and wenches to having intellectual discussions with his wife. So, like any intelligent woman, Ealine decided to 'give him the bird' – in the shape of a starling she had taught to speak and which she sent winging over the fields to tell her father of her ill treatment.

As a result the armies of the two warriors met in a fearful battle at the ford which still bears Bren's name. He was killed outright and Horsa mortally wounded, but Ealine was carried home in triumph in time to attend her father's funeral. The mound over the grave where Horsa and his favourite war-horse were buried was named after him, being corrupted to 'Horsenden' over the years. Ealine and her mother retired in their widow's weeds to the forest nearby where they devoted themselves to study.

But some say that Horsa's giant steed can still be heard pacing around his sepulchre and the shadowy form of the dead warrior has been seen on nights when 'the pale moon illumines the hill and the white mists curl upward from the vale at its foot'.

Pinner 🐌

Any mention of Pinner conjures up the familiar picture of the village High Street with its fine timber framed houses and small shops lining the way to the splendid 14th century parish church of St John the Baptist. This is its old world charm, but beneath lies a modern bustling suburb, as prosperous now as it was in Elizabethan days.

How Pinner came by its name is not known for certain but, since 'ora' means river bank, it is generally assumed that this was once 'Pinna's settlement on the banks of the river'. Documents of 1232 concerning a certain Alfwin, who succeeded to his father's house and estate of 200 acres of land, refer to it as 'Pinnora'. Although agriculture was the main occupation of the area, other local industries grew up over the years. Chalk excavation was one, a chalk pit near Waxwell Lane is recorded as early as 1648 and the industry expanded and thrived until around 1887 when the pits were

Pinner

closed for economic reasons. A reminder came to light in 1932 when a disused shaft 110 ft deep, with galleries at the bottom running towards Waxwell Lane, was discovered in a field off Pinner Hill Road.

The area of West Middlesex lying between Pinner, Uxbridge and Brentford is where the London clay outcrops and was used extensively before the motor car age to grow hay to feed the large number of horses stabled in Central London, the district being known as the Hay Country. In 1885 a new era began and the Metropolitan railway reached across the hay fields to Pinner, the first train arriving on Whit Monday, 25th May. The line through Pinner village came under the ownership of the Metropolitan and Great Central Joint Committee in 1906 and was electrified between Harrow on the Hill and Rickmansworth in 1905. All trains had first class accommodation until 1941. Two Pullman cars were operated by the Metropolitan railway but ceased at the outbreak of the Second World War. A favourite Pullman was the midnight express from Baker Street, very popular with theatregoers who could be served with drinks and snacks on their way home to Pinner. The Pullman supplement was one shilling on top of the first class return fare of 2/3d. Alas, Pinner is now merely an ordinary stop on the London Underground system.

In the 1930s the Hay Country was re-named 'Metroland' and the phrase 'Live in Metroland' was coined. A couple could have bought a house in Ruislip, Wembley or Pinner for £350 (a three bedroomed villa) or £425 (a four bedroomed residence)! Housing estates sprang up. To the east of Pinner High Street the Cecil Park Estate, an estate agent's brochure spoke of 'Good class semi-detached houses to be let, rents from £50 to £75 per annum, charmingly situated and within a few minutes walk of Pinner Village and the Metropolitan Railway Station'. To the west the Cuckoo Hill Estate offered, 'The City Man's Ideal Residential Suburb. Superior Freehold Villas and Spacious Building Plots for Sale. Houses built to your own ideas and designs. Eight minutes walk from Pinner Station (Metro)'. Northwood Hills Station was opened in 1933 and soon the houses began to rise along Joel Street and Pinner Road. And so modern Pinner was born.

Pinner parish church stands dominant at the top of the High Street. It was rebuilt in 1321 as a chapel of the mother church at Harrow. Local materials, flint especially, were used. The south porch and tower of three stages were added in the 15th century and the large cross in 1637. Pinner remained part of the parish of Harrow until 1766 when it became a separate parish. In spite of the south porch being drastically restored in 1880 and other changes including a 1958 facelift to the interior, the church retains its dignified simplicity. The church has also inherited a splendid 400 year old tradition. The eight bells, installed in 1771, can be rung in set sequences to a fixed rhythm known as change ringing, which is an exercise which has become an art in itself. The ring prior to that date was known as 'The Pinner Old Five', and a church inventory dated 1553 refers to 'belles'. Pause and think of their history as the sound of the bells wafts down the High Street for Tuesday evening practice, a wedding or a Sunday service.

In the churchyard, on the north side of the church, you will see a simple wooden headboard, beneath which lies the body of William Skenelby, the village Methuselah, who was buried there on 10th November 1775, aged 118. The Pinner air evidently suited him! Near the south porch is a 20 ft high monument known as the Loudon Monument. This is quite famous as the 'coffin above ground crypt', as the inscription tablets protruding from it remind people of a coffin. It was erected by John Claudius Loudon, a celebrated horticulturist, in memory of his parents.

To the left of the church in Paines Lane stands Heywood House, originally known as Equestrian House where two of the drivers of the London–Pinner coach lived. In 1878 a Judge Barber bought the house, added the gabled part and then renamed it 'Ye Cocoa Tree'. As a temperance tavern it became quite popular for Sunday school treats and day trips. People picnicked in the large gardens and children enjoyed donkey rides. The sign showed a tree with cups of cocoa hanging from it. Further along Paines Lane is the cemetery where Horatia Nelson Ward, daughter of Admiral Lord Nelson and Lady Hamilton is buried. Their granddaughter, Eleanor Ward, who was run over outside the Queen's Head in the High Street and died in a neighbouring shop, is also buried there.

Pinner's 16th century black and white High Street, with its 24 listed buildings, owes its unusual width and character to the fact that for centuries it has served as a market place and as a site for the annual fair. The fair goes back to the days of Edward III who granted a charter in 1336 to the then

Archbishop of Canterbury and his successors for ever. To guarantee the continuity small fairs have even been held during war years, so that for more than 650 years Pinner's annual fair has continued to attract the crowds. It is now held each year on the Wednesday following the Spring Bank Holiday Monday and on that day all traffic ceases down the High Street and Bridge Street and thousands of people flock into Pinner from the surrounding districts.

The Queen's Head is the most attractive old inn in the High Street and its origins date back to the late 16th century. It is thought that the original 'Queen' may have been Queen Philippa, wife of Edward III, although it was Queen Anne who changed horses there in 1705 and has been portrayed on the inn sign ever since. The annual Pinner wheelbarrow race finishes at the Queen's Head. The race is the modern counterpart of the old plough races dating back to the 14th century. The course is from the common via The Oddfellows, The George, The Victory and The Hand in Hand, with half a pint of beer to be drunk at each.

Pinner has an unusual war memorial. In 1947 West House and its park were purchased by public subscription as a memorial to the fallen in both world wars. The Memorial Park, known locally as 'The Duck Park', gives endless pleasure to children and residents of all ages.

Modern Pinner has three major problems, water, parking and property developers! After torrential rain the river Pinn overflows and floods the bottom of the High Street and a number of residential areas. A scheme to improve matters is long overdue.

New residents find Pinner a friendly area, and it cannot be faulted for convenience, for they can be in the City in half an hour using the Metropolitan Line.

Pinner in many ways seems to have the best of both worlds, of town and country. If you stroll half way up Wakeham's Hill and turn left down a grassy footpath to the kissing gate you will see two wooden seats. On one is a plaque which says, 'In memory of Molly Weir's mother, who thought Pinner the Bonniest place'. What an epitaph!

Ponders End

Some say that, centuries ago, a certain Mr Ponder lived in the last little dwelling at the edge of the fields. Travellers seeking directions were told to ask again at Ponder's End.

Ponders End has come a long way since then. Arable farming thrived and fine residences were built. Among them, in the 16th century, the home of the Bishop and Earls of Lincoln. Durants Arbour, built on the site of the manor house of Durants, played host on occasion to James I, as well as to the infamous Judge Jeffreys on his way to London.

Ponders End is very proud of its family owned flour mill. The mill, which was built in the 17th century, is an efficiently run, flourishing business which has moved with the times. It has been owned by the Wright family for over 100 years.

In the 19th century, the railway came steaming through the countryside. The station – now British Rail, carrying the public to and from the City – was constructed, and brought passengers and freight. Along the tracks came coal to the pioneers of the gas works and gas company, now British Gas.

Towards the end of the century, the council purchased allotments. Some of these are still going strong and, by hard work, producing fine vegetables.

St Matthew's Church school was built in 1838. Later, St Matthew's beautiful parish church came into being, its foundation stone laid in 1900. Alongside is the church hall.

Ponders End has been fortunate in having the river Lea close by to carry its industrial goods and raw materials. Did its nickname 'Ponders Plonk' arise from when children throwing pebbles into the river, revelled in the noise they made hitting the water?

The farms, orchards and nurseries of yesteryear have now given way to housing estates and tower block flats. The industrial areas are mostly thriving, albeit in different ways from earlier times.

During the Second World War, Ponders End suffered its share of attacks from enemy bombers, because of its closeness to London, to the movements on the river Lea, the marshalling yards at Ponders End lock and the Royal Small Arms factory at Enfield lock.

There is no village green but, coming along the High Street, gates lead into the park where it is pleasant to sit and admire the flower beds. From the deserted bandstand, can there be heard the phantom strains of a bygone brass band? Perhaps there will come the sounds of a steel band filling the air, as there is now a multi-racial community. There are caring groups for all who live in the area.

There is a well attended mosque and many places of Christian worship, and where there's a church, there's a pub, so they say! There are several in the High Street including The Goat, which dates back to around 1752 when it was a coaching inn and the surrounding lands belonged to the aforementioned Earls of Lincoln. The coaches changed horses here on their way from the City of London to Cambridge. Part of the cobblestoned stableyard floor remains to this day. This congenial tavern now sees London Tranports buses pass by, some to nearby Ponders End bus garage.

It has been unkindly said by some, and heartily contradicted by most, that 'Ponders End was the last place God made' – last but not least!

Roxeth 🪶

Long before civilisation engulfed Roxeth, its wooded heights provided an attractive haven for a great variety of birds. The socially minded rooks found conditions to their liking and many large rookeries existed in the region (and still do). Rooks were well established between the 9th and 11th centuries when Vikings frequently raided Mercia and their word for rook was 'hroc', while 'seath' meant 'spring'. These words gradually combined to spell 'Roxy' or 'Roxeth' – 'a place where rooks drink'. The river became Roxbourne – the stream of rooks.

There is an old country belief that rooks are to be 'told' of the death of a landowner. The new owner is obliged to stand beneath the trees and announce the bad news to the occupants of nearby rookeries.

Not only the rooks found the area around the river Roxbourne to their liking. It seems that the earliest Roxeth community also settled in close proximity to this convenient source of fresh water. A scattered settlement was well established by the 14th century.

Roxeth had several common fields, Newton, Middle and Dobbs fields. Dobbs was famed for the quality of its rich corn and as the site of the local mill. Newton field produced a high quality hay considered to be the best in the kingdom and which fetched high prices. Over the centuries Newton field has been a Roman site, a Saxon tithing, a medieval common, a Victorian sewage farm and latterly a modern suburb. The boundaries of Newton field are thought to date back to AD 74. The Newton and the Dobbs field were separated by a track known as 'The Long Mile', which later became Eastcote Lane.

At the junction of Field End Road with Eastcote Lane there is a traffic roundabout at a place called Ascot Bushe, on the bank of the Roxbourne. At this point on the map was embedded one of the eight stones which marked the ancient boundaries of Roxeth, which was re-sited by Harrow Council on the occasion of Roxeth's 11th centenary (845–1945).

Until the First World War, Roxeth's neighbouring villages, namely Harrow, Pinner, Northolt, Ruislip and Eastcote, were separated by tracts of unspoilt countryside through which ran picturesque streams and brooks protected by surrounding woodland. Narrow country lanes wound through the fields to several rich farms. But in June 1903 the District Line railway came to Roxeth and during the next three decades London crept slowly westwards, engulfing most of the farms and other attractive rural features.

In 1855 John Chapman began making gas in a factory in Northolt Road. Rural Roxeth was able to boast of gas-lit houses long before its urban neighbours.

In 1872 the Harrow Gaslight and Coke Co was formed and within a year became Harrow District Gas Company, with John Chapman as vice chairman. In 1894 the Harrow company amalgamated with neighbouring areas. The large gasholder was put up between 1928 and 1931. As time went by the company became part of the North Thames Gas Board.

The gas works are no longer used for making or holding town gas since the area was converted to Natural Gas. In modern times the letters NO were painted on top of the gasometer as a guide to planes following an overhead flight-path to Northolt Aerodrome. There was a near collision over the gasometer in 1970 before these letters were added, when one pilot had become confused and taken the wrong flight-path.

In the late 19th century there were few shops. Davidge's sold papers, sweets and tobacco. Next to Davidge's shop was Shearlock's the Grocer's. His shop always smelled interesting, with sides of bacon hanging up, large hams on china stands and tins of biscuits with glass lids, all very tempting. In the corner of the shop was a barrel of treacle, which was sold loose.

Davidge's shop was nearly opposite the Three Horses which had a fair sized pond by it. The licensee was one Charlie Atkins, a huge man, reputed to weigh over 32 stone.

From time to time there were drag hunts in Roxeth. This always caused a stir and was a brave sight as the hunt proceeded down the Northolt Road, or down the Long Mile to Eastcote. There were also staghounds kept in Waldron's Yard by officers from Windsor, and on one famous occasion a stag ran up the road and took refuge in a cottage.

The organ grinder used to stop in the village and Mrs Davidge would give him a twist of snuff. He would let the children turn the handle of the organ. Sometimes he would bring a Russian bear with a chain round its neck, and the poor animal would dance to the music.

Horace Fleet, of Stanley Road was a keen balloonist, and kept his hot air balloon in a big shed on waste ground. He and a brave woman named Florence used to balloon from the field. The balloon was so patched it never went very far, but the children used to race under it across the field until it came to rest.

Sanger's Circus came annually and was held in one of the fields. It was heralded by a procession, frequently led by Lord George Sanger, and included 'Buffalo Bill and his Painted Redskins', a bear in a cage and a few other animals, some clowns and a fairy queen high on the top of a float pulled by horses. There was a half day holiday at Roxeth school for the circus.

In the mid 19th century, Roxeth needed a church of her own because of the population growth in the area. The then vicar of Harrow the Rev J. H. Cunningham, took steps to provide this daughter church and Christ Church was built in 1862, of flint and stone. The architect was Sir Gilbert Scott.

112

The name links it with the monks of Christ Church, Canterbury, the medieval manor of Roxeth having been in the fee of the Archbishops of Canterbury. The church provided parish entertainments such as penny readings and magic lantern shows. It also ran a soup kitchen in the bad weather and a bread and a coal fund for the needy – coal was supplied at 4d per hundredweight.

Sunday school treats were some of the great occasions of the year, and the following account is taken from the parish magazine of 1892 – 'The children mustered at Roxeth Corner at 5.30 am with banners and a bright display of flags. After falling into procession, the children stood with 'hats off' while the curate said a prayer. Off they would walk to Harrow station. At the hospital a halt was made whilst the children sang a verse of a hymn, usually at the request of one of the patients. Harrow station was reached at 6.30 am. The train steamed into the station . . . Brighton was reached at 9 o'clock and here the enjoyment of 180 children and 150 parents and friends was unbounded.'

The story of Roxeth church is now over 100 years old and the immediate surroundings have changed immensely, but from the entrance on Roxeth Hill can still be seen the peaceful oasis of the old Victorian village.

Roxeth school is probably the second oldest continuing school in Harrow, opened in 1851. The pretty Gothic building was dedicated by Lord Shaftesbury to his 16 year old son Anthony Francis Henry Ashley who died on 31st May, 1849 while a pupil at Harrow School. There is a plaque inside the school recording this. An infant block was built onto the main block in 1854, with lodging for the headmistress. The number of children in the infant school steadily rose, so that in 1864 there were 50 infants.

Discipline was strict, all were expected to behave in an orderly manner. Disobedience and playing truant were punished with the strap. Children could start school at three years old, the only stipulation for entrance being that the child was 'dry'. School cost two pennies per week. Mid-day meals were prepared as 'cookery lessons' under the care of a teacher at a range in a small kitchen. Needlework was an important lesson and the older pupils undertook orders for the gentry. Pupils seldom wrote on paper and exercise books were unknown. Everyone wrote on a slate.

The first Roxeth hospital was founded in 1866, when two cottages were leased on Roxeth Hill, a little lower down than the school. These two cottages were converted into a home of nine beds but it soon became apparent that this was not suitable for the purpose. Drainage was practically non-existent. In 1868 the landlady gave the trustees notice to quit so the board had to look out for an alternative. Lack of funds was a problem but a Mr Charles Leaf, a great local benefactor, offered to purchase the land if money for the building could be raised. In December 1872 the second hospital of eleven beds was opened. Besides the wards it had an operating room and a dispensary. Conveyance to hospital was by a two-wheeled stretcher.

From about the second quarter of the 20th century, Roxeth, as a living community with its own name was changed. The suburban areas of South Harrow, West Harrow and Rayners Lane were artificially superimposed upon the ancient village and its three adjoining fields. Organisations like the Trust which have helped to preserve Harrow-on-the-Hill have not had similar success in Roxeth, but Roxeth's history cannot be overlooked.

Ruislip

At the heart of Ruislip village is the Manor Farm which has a history dating back to Saxon times, or even earlier as Roman fragments have been found. The earliest known lord of the manor was Wluuard Wit, a wealthy baron in the favour of Edward the Confessor in the 11th century, who had estates in various parts of the country as well as Middlesex.

However, with the arrival in England of William the Conqueror, Wluuard Wit was dispossessed, and the manor of Ruislip passed to a Norman knight called Ernulf de Hesdin. He went on a Crusade to the Holy Land in 1096, leaving the manor of Ruislip in the hands of the Abbot of Bec in Normandy on condition that the monks would pray forever for his soul.

It is very certain that these monks built a priory at Manor Farm. Today a moat surrounds on three sides a mound which may well have had a motte and bailey castle of wooden construction built upon it in Norman times. For the next three centuries the monks continued to farm the land, increasing their landholding and preserving its prosperity. By the late 13th century they had a manor house with chapel and by the 14th century the house was much extended and contained valuable silver, linen and furniture.

The 'manor of Ruyslepe' passed in the 15th century to the provost and scholars of King's College, Cambridge. For the next 450 years they leased the manor to a succession of people. During the 17th century the Earl of Salisbury was leaseholder, and the manor then passed to the Hawtreys and their descendants until the late 19th century.

A new manor house had been erected in the early 16th century, oak-framed infilled with brick and roofed with tiles locally made. Until the 1930s it was the farmhouse of the manor, but in 1932 under pressure from local people King's College gave the Manor Farm with its outbuildings to the Ruislip and Northwood District Council for community use.

All the buildings are well preserved today by the London Borough of Hillingdon and are popular venues for many local organisations. The two most interesting buildings apart from the farmhouse are the Great Barn, which is weatherboarded with a tiled roof and is thought to date from the 13th century, and the Little Barn of the 16th century now the Ruislip public library. The former stables is now a boys club, the 18th century cow-shed is now a Guide hut, and the cow byre, a modern replica of one burnt down in 1976, now houses art exhibitions and a tea room.

At the corner of the High Street and Eastcote Road stands St Martin's church, which dates from about 1250. It has beautiful roof carvings and stained glass windows and the font, made of Purbeck marble, is 11th century. On the inside wall of the north aisle hangs the Bread Cupboard which, from 1697 to 1955 held loaves of bread which were given on Sundays to poor parishioners. This charitable gift was instituted by Jeremiah Bright, son of a vicar of Ruislip, who prospered in the Leathersellers' Company. The cupboard is inscribed, 'The gift of Jeremiah Bright, of London, being 2/- worth of bread to be distributed by ye Minister and Churchwardens to the Poor every Sunday. For Ever. Anno Domini 1697.' During the Second World War, a food parcel replaced the rationed loaf! North of the churchyard are 16th century cottages which were once Church houses, became almshouses and are now splendidly restored as dwellings.

The old post office, at the top of the High Street, is 16th century as are the shops on one side of the road and The Swan public house on the other. Seen from the rear, their antiquity is confirmed despite later extensions at the front. The shop beside the lychgate, once an ale house, still has its stone staircase and old fireplace, and the modern estate agent's opposite conceals a 16th century store-room. The village pump, though not in its original position, still graces the High Street.

In 1904 the advent of the Metropolitan railway with a station at Ruislip brought a great diversity of private and council housing. There are still working farms in the area, and being so close to Northolt airport, there is a floating

Manor Farm House, Ruislip

population of British and Allied service families. Where the road from Ruislip meets the A40, stands the Polish War Memorial which commemorates the sacrifice made by their gallant airmen during the Battle of Britain and afterwards. Civic amenities include churches of several denominations, a fine library and indoor swimming pool and sheltered homes for the elderly, as well as a golf course and driving range for enthusiasts and a world famous shooting school.

Earliest productions by the Ruislip Dramatic Society were staged in 'The Tin Tabernacle' (now defunct) in Bury Street and the old Rivoli Cinema, converted for stage use. Here the men's dressing room was in the barber's shop over the road, while the ladies changed in a marquee in the car park. The shadows produced by the makeshift lighting often attracted a

117

larger audience than the actual performance! The Ruislip & District Musical and Dramatic Society now puts on shows of very high calibre at the Winston Churchill Hall.

Ruislip was originally arable and woodland, the trees being mainly oak and hornbeam. From the woods, timber was requisitioned for the construction of the Tower of London, Windsor Castle and the Palace of Westminster. Thanks to the herculean efforts of local residents over the years, Copse (formerly Coppice) Wood, Mad Bess Wood and Park Wood ('a park of wild beasts' in the Domesday Book) are all now owned by Hillingdon Borough Council. Within their bounds lie one of the first natural history reserves in Southern England, a bird sanctuary and a Lido for fishing, sailing and water-skiing.

So, here is a thriving, vital community, proud of its ancient history, in step with present day professional and business concerns. In its heart, Ruislip retains its village identity and it will never become a dormitory satellite for Greater London.

Shepperton

It is easy to find Shepperton on any map which shows the course of the river Thames, just look for the most southerly point and there it lies, cradled in the curve. Referred to in the Domesday Book as Scepertone, its 900 acres were once valued at just £7. The name meant 'Shepherd Town', and even today many sheep graze on the banks of the Queen Mary reservoir, which was the largest of its kind in the world when it was completed in 1925. To achieve this, sacrifices had to be made, and the little hamlet of Astlam was 'drowned' during construction. There are many reservoirs in the area and it is said that together with the Thames and its tributaries and flooded disused gravel workings, there is more water here than in the Norfolk Broads!

SHEPPERTON

Shepperton War Memorial

119

A hoard of Iron Age coins was found in Shepperton in 1950 and in more recent years, traces of timber and mud houses used by Iron Age people. Roman weapons and coins and an early Saxon cemetery have also been found.

The area close to Church Square is that most often written about, and it seems to have changed little in recent years. The church of St Nicholas, built in 1614, replaced an earlier church which was badly damaged by flood from the river in 1605. It is unique in that it has two outside staircases and a very unusual gallery. The old public houses, the Anchor and the King's Head stand on either side of Church Square. Nell Gwynne is said to have lodged in the King's Head, and Lord Nelson and Lady Hamilton to have visited the Anchor. The Square itself was well known for the illegal bare-fisted fights staged there in the late 18th and early 19th centuries, the large curve of the river affording ample opportunity for the participants to make their escape over the water should the Law threaten to intervene.

The Revd William Russell, rector of Shepperton for 53 years until 1870, transformed the village, his most notable achievement being the erection of the village Church school in 1833, an all-age school. The railway arrived in Shepperton in 1864. In 1982 one of the trains forgot it was the end of the line, and tried to continue its journey down the High Road!

Famous residents, or long-stay visitors have included Charles Dickens, H. G. Wells, Jerome K. Jerome, Gilbert and Sullivan (D'Oyly Carte Island visitors). Queen Victoria's tutor, Thomas Steward, is buried in the village cemetery, as is Thomas Love Peacock. Peacock's baby daughter, Margaret, is buried near St Nicholas' church, and her headstone is engraved with a touching poem written by her father.

'Long night succeeds thy little day
Oh blighted blossom can it be,
That this gray stone and grassy clay
Have closed our anxious care of thee?'

In recent times, famous film stars have lived in the village, or lodged at many of the inns, Judy Garland, Charlie Chaplin, Elizabeth Taylor to name but a few.

In 1810 an Act of Parliament empowered the Corporation of London to erect four pound locks, one each at Chertsey Bridge, Shepperton, Sunbury and Teddington. The Walton Bridge end of the village was famed for the Cowey Stakes, said to have been erected in the river in an attempt to stop the Romans from crossing, and on the shore was an area known as Gibbetts Corner, where the last public hanging was carried out, possibly in the 1870s. Who knows, history is still in the making, and one day it may be famous for having the longest standing 'temporary' bridge over the river!

Shepperton Green ✀

Shepperton Green is a small but very friendly village. As with a lot of older communities, it has developed from a mainly agricultural area and it was through here that many a shepherd herded his flock en route to London. One of the main walk ways for the animals is still called Sheep Walk . . . forever immortalized!

From a small turning off Sheep Walk you can reach the village school and once there, delve into history, since its name 'Saxon' derived from the remains of our ancestors which were found when the foundations were being dug. Some of these artefacts are kept there and can be viewed when on a visit to the school.

Older members of Shepperton Green village have had to

suffer the dust and rumblings connected with gravel pits when they were being worked, since this area is quite prolific in this commodity, but these days the village is reaping benefits from those years gone by as the now disused pits have been turned into beautiful lakes teeming with birds and wildlife and many different species of fish including some very good trout. Many a troubled mind could be calmed by the tranquil view from the water's edge watching the sailing or fishing, and it is a joy to behold the Canada Geese with their babies.

There is no need to go thirsty here, as there is an abundance of public houses, the most obvious one in Shepperton Green being The Bull. This can be easily found at the top end of the aforementioned Sheep Walk. Among the many stars who have tippled a pint or two here, it must not be overlooked that the Duke of Windsor used to visit quite regularly in his youth. The walls have also rung to the tunes of Tessy O'Shea and her ukelele. Bordering the village are the famous Shepperton film studios (actually in Littleton) and the Queen Mary reservoir.

One local resident remembers life in the village in the 1930s. 'Squires Road, along with several others in this area was not "made-up" and it flooded and became quite muddy when it rained. It had grass verges then and I can recall several varieties of wild flowers, including delicate harebells, growing among the grass. There were very few cars around and you could buy milk from a man who drove a horse and cart.

We had cess-pits in the gardens, and not until the late 1930s were we put on to main drainage and the roads made-up. We were not afraid to play in the road as children, as there was little danger. The roads reflected the past in their names, such as Wood Road, Watersplash Road, Sheep Walk, Ash Road (after the river Ash), Squires Bridge Road and

Squires Road (after the squire of the manor), Pool End and Fairview Drive.

We walked a lot when I was a child, and the road to Laleham was a pleasant tree lined road. A turning off Laleham Road was Littleton Lane, an interesting road to traverse, with sloe bushes that were a mass of white blossom in the spring and often covered with bitter damson-like fruit in the summer. Halfway down Littleton Lane on the left hand side was a natural spring that flowed across the fields on the left, first making a large marshy area that abounded with "milk-maids", kingcups and cowslips. Further on this became the stream that flowed across the fields at the bottom of Fairview Drive, where we caught sticklebacks and minnows, and then on to Pool End in Sheep Walk and on to Shepperton itself, running past the Three Horseshoes pub and under the road by the war memorial, emerging on the other side eventually to flow into the river Thames. Part of this beautiful stream was lost when gravel pits started to be worked and the rest has almost disappeared owing to the building of the M3 motorway which cut Shepperton Green off from Shepperton, by causing the road to go over the motorway.

The large gravel pit on the left hand side of Littleton Lane has been there for a long time and is used now for sailing, wind surfing and even skin diving. The new inhabitants in the area call these pits, lakes, and they may have various interesting flora and fauna, but it is sad to think of the days when these fields were rich with grass, buttercups, wild roses and hawthorn bushes as well as various varieties of large trees. There you could see many wild birds including owls and kingfishers, and where in the late summer you could collect huge mushrooms.

We even had a tramp who lived wild at the corner where several fields met, going into a home during the winter months. He was known as "Musha Smallpiece" and I must admit I was a little scared of him.

We could walk down Firview Drive, across the stream and over the fields, crossing about four stiles and coming out at the bottom of Littleton Lane, and then across the Chertsey Road, through another stile in the hedge and across Chertsey Meads to the river. There was a bathing hut where you could change into swimming costumes and swim in the river Thames.

The river was a great attraction as it still is now. You could paddle, swim and fish, or hire a small boat for an hour or two for 2/6d, a dinghy, punt or skiff.'

Sipson ✺

Bounded by the M4 motorway in the north, Heathrow airport in the south, Harmondsworth in the west and Harlington in the east, Sipson is on what was once the big Middlesex heathland, Hounslow Heath.

The village was in the past mainly agricultural, referred to at one time as a 'fruity' village, no doubt due to the amount of orchards and market gardens. The ancient names of Shepiston and Sibbeston originally meant Sibwine's farm. This name of Shepiston is now in use again, since the M4 motorway cut across the main road to form Shepiston Lane, a local road to Pinkwell and Harlington.

Things have changed so much in this area since 1945. The biggest change has without doubt been the building of Heathrow airport, and in its wake the M4 motorway and spur road to the airport, and The Post House and Excelsior hotels. The farms and market gardens have gone, or are put to other uses. The large houses of the 'grower' families with one exception have also been demolished. The Wild's house known as The Vineries (or unofficially as 'Holy City' because

124

of the text on the front) has given way to Vineries Close, The Gables to Kenwood Close. On these sites smaller houses have been built to accommodate the ever changing population of airport and hotel workers. However, that was not to be the fate of the Phelps' Georgian Sipson House, which after years of neglect has been restored and refurbished and is now the offices of the CAA. Unfortunately the Welcome Coffee Tavern, built by the Wild and Robbins families in 1897 as a counter attraction to public houses is today in a deplorable state.

Talking to long time residents one hears of some of the events and 'doings' of Sipson before the Second World War. There were some pretty little cottages in the village, one row was called Sixteen Row and the other Eighteen Row. On the walk to West Drayton, the trees used to meet over the road. There was only one bungalow and the Plough public house on this road and a lovely little stream ran across it. At one time everyone in the village worked for Wild and Robbins, market gardeners, and lived in houses owned by the firm. There were only two cars in the village, one owned by Mr Wild and the other by Mr Robbins. Mrs Wild drove a pony and trap and when children were skipping in the road they had to let the rope down for her to go over it.

The Three Magpies public house on the Bath Road once had a pond at the back of it. In 1918 a fete was held there to celebrate the Armistice. Flowers were sold at the roadside outside the Magpies, especially around Ascot Week, catching the passing traffic trade along the Bath Road. One can still see this practice today and on the Colnbrook by-pass at weekends. Fetes were also held on the land occupied now by the Excelsior Hotel, and the village children used to cut across this field on their way to the Sipson and Heathrow school. This school was demolished in 1968 and a new Heathrow school built in Harmondsworth Lane.

Smith's jam factory on the Sipson Road has gone now, but

in its time local children could earn 1½d per basket picking gooseberries etc from the Walled Garden Farm in Sipson Lane. Near the jam factory stood the forge, which was part of the Wild & Robbins firm, but not exclusively for their use. There was in later years a caravan works also on this site, now replaced by houses. On the opposite side of Sipson Road was the Home Farm estate. The corner was known as Bomer Corner and tramps could often be seen taking a rest there and having a 'brew-up' when walking from Hillingdon workhouse to Staines. The name is still in use having been given to Bomer Close, a 1950s housing development.

Other villages around this area have disappeared, buildings, houses, cottages and farms swallowed up by the airport. Very few now remember Kings Arbour, Perry Oakes is now the water works and not much more, and Hatton is a name on the Piccadilly Tube line. One thing does remain of old Heathrow, the barrel of a cannon and a plaque to mark the end of a base line that had been measured across Hounslow Heath in 1784, as part of a trigonometric survey made by the father of Ordnance Survey, Major-General William Roy. This can be seen still on the airport Northside near the taxi park.

Southall

Southall possesses a very picturesque Elizabethan building known as the Manor House. There are very few of these houses left in or around London and it is closely connected to the ancient church of St Mary the Virgin at Norwood Green. In 1543, Henry VIII had received the manor of Hayes, Norwood and Southall from Archbishop Cranmer in exchange for lands in Kent. The mulberry tree still in the grounds was planted in Henry's time as were other trees still in existence.

Built in the 16th century under the name of 'Wrenn's',

Richard Awsiter made various improvements when he bought the house in 1587 and substantial changes were made during the 18th and 19th centuries. The timber framed house is most beautiful. The house was not included in the sale of the manor to Agatha Child in 1756 and remained in the Awsiter family until 1821 when it was bought by William Welch. William Thomas, inventor of the lock-stitch sewing machine, bought the house in the 1880s. In 1885 he provided hot dinners daily during the winter for the children whose fathers were out of work because the extreme cold had forced the brickfields to close.

The council bought the manor house in 1913 and it is now used as offices for the Southall Chamber of Commerce who have paid for much of the restoration work, including the fireplace in the central hall attributed to Grinling Gibbons.

A large tithe barn about 360 years old stood in the south corner of the grounds of the manor and in the 19th century the occupants of the house allowed a priest to use it for mass on Sundays. This soon became the original Roman Catholic church in Southall and was consecrated as St Anselm's.

The stocks were placed a few hundred yards from the main entrance of the Manor House and this is the site of the now Featherstone Road. Unfortunately these were destroyed by vandals at the beginning of the last century.

Southall Market is historic, having been granted a royal charter by William III to sell cattle. Francis Merrick, a great benefactor to the people of Southall, applied to the King for the charter in 1698 and this was immediately granted. The original charter is in the Central Library although it has now lost its seal. The market is still open for cattle, trading on Wednesdays and sometimes donkeys are also traded, which is now rare in this country. On Fridays and Saturdays the market is open for general trading and access can be gained from the Uxbridge Road.

The most distinguished residents of Southall were the Martin brothers. Their pottery became world famous. In

1877 they opened their first kiln in Southall in Havelock Road. Most of their equipment was transported by barge on the canal. There is a small selection of their pottery in the Southall library, but the main collection is now housed in Ealing Town Hall.

Staines 🐝

The Thames has always been the most important feature of Staines and remains so today. The Romans called their settlement here Ad Pontes – 'the bridges' and since this was the first crossing upstream from London Bridge, the settlement was of considerable importance for trade and military purposes. There have been several bridges at Staines since Roman times and the present bridge was designed by John and George Rennie of Waterloo Bridge fame and opened by King William IV in 1832.

The name Staines comes from the Anglo-Saxon for stone. In the Anglo-Saxon Chronicle the settlement was known as Stana, while it appears in the Domesday survey as Stanes.

There is a pleasant riverside walk along the towpath, and near the Thames Lodge Hotel (once the Packhorse Hotel) there are two cottages called 'Hook on' and 'Shoot off'. Here the towpath crosses from the Middlesex bank to the Surrey bank, and the horses had to gallop with their barges to give the barges sufficient impetus to shoot over to the other side of the Thames, where they were then hooked on to the horses after they had crossed the road bridge. There are some large vertical iron rollers near the cottages which were used to assist this process. Boating and fishing are very popular leisure activities on this stretch of the Thames, and some working tugs and barges are still to be seen.

During the third week in July each year the Swan Uppers

128

arrive in small boats on their journey from Southwark to Henley, marking the beaks of all the cygnets with the same marks as the parent swans. Two thirds of the swans belong to the Queen and the rest belong to the Worshipful Company of Vintners and the worshipful Company of Dyers.

Just beyond Staines bridge in Ashby Recreation Ground stands the London Stone, marking what was once the most westerly point of the City of London's jurisdiction over the Thames (this is actually a replica stone, the original stands in the foyer of Staines library protected from the weather). It bears the inscription 'God preserve ye Cittye of London AD 1285' and a coat of arms. Until 1857, when the jurisdiction was taken over by Thames Conservancy, the Lord Mayor of London made an annual visit by barge to the Stone. There are still tax posts to be seen around Staines bearing the City of London coat of arms and in use from 1861 to 1890 as marker posts for the payment of coal and wine duty to the City of London.

Staines features in Jerome K. Jerome's book *Three Men in a Boat* in a description of the signing of Magna Carta. 'King John has slept at Duncroft Hall, and all the day before the little town of Staines has echoed to the clang of armed men...'. Whether or not King John did actually sleep at Duncroft Hall, it was from Staines that the Barons and their men rode out to meet with King John at Runnymede. There, on 15th June 1215, Magna Carta was signed.

The 290 acres of Staines Moor was still wild and lonely, and the Moor is listed as a Site of Special Scientific Interest with several species of rare flora and fauna, including a rare type of earthworm.

Alan Ayckbourn and Christine Keeler were one time pupils at Kingston Road primary school, and Richard Murdoch lived in Staines. Murdoch Close, near the railway station, is named after him.

Lagonda cars were made in Staines from 1906 to 1947.

Linoleum was first produced here in 1862 and production grew rapidly, only ceasing in the early 1970s when the factory was transferred to Scotland.

Brewing started in Staines in the 18th century and was developed by Thomas Ashby, who gave the town the Ashby Recreation Ground. The buildings from Thomas Harris's brewery are now known as Staines Oast House and are used by Staines Adult Education Institute. Courage Breweries now own the site of Ashby's Brewery and they have recently built a magnificent new Head Office on this site.

Tragedy came to Staines on 18th June 1972 when a Trident taking off from Heathrow airport crashed near the A30, narrowly missing houses and killing all 118 passengers and crew.

Stanmore

The history of Stanmore common is known to go back beyond the time of the Romans, who had a settlement on the slopes of what is now Brockley Hill following the defeat of the local tribe of Cassi. In fact one of the ponds on the common is still named 'Caesar's Pond'. The name Stanmore is believed to have been derived following the Saxon destruction of this settlement when, because of the débris which covered acres of land, it was known as 'the stones by the mere'.

Over the centuries it developed into Great Stanmore and Little Stanmore, the former being the area around St John's church at the bottom of Stanmore Hill, the latter being around St Lawrence's church. The track which connected them is now known as Marsh Lane.

At the turn of this century Stanmore was still mainly an area of farmland and pasture with a few large houses and, of course, the cottages of the farm labourers. The parish reputedly consisted of about 1,500 acres of land and 14 acres of water and was thought to be a healthy environment as the villages are over 200 ft above sea level and the common over 470 ft above sea level.

Of the large houses surviving to the present day, Stanmore Hall is a listed building and so protected for posterity. Bentley Priory, once the home of Queen Adelaide, was purchased in the late 18th century by the 1st Marquis of Abercorn who commissioned Sir John Soane to rebuild the house. It has been occupied by the RAF since before the Second World War, during which Lord Dowding and Fighter Command used it as their headquarters.

The pilot who shot down the first Zeppelin of the First World War over Cuffley is celebrated by having a public house named after him as one leaves Stanmore for Harrow Weald – Leafe Robinson.

Of the two parish churches, St Lawrence's is best known, perhaps, for George Frederick Handel having been the organist there under the patronage of the Duke of Chandos, until 1721. Few people are aware of the fact that the organ's black keys are white and the white are, in fact, black! The church's painted ceiling on which are depicted eight miracles, the three graces, the four evangelists and St Peter and St Paul, was executed by Laguerre and at least four Venetian artists. This was restored to its former glory in 1986. Only the old tower of the original church remains following demolition by the Duke of Chandos. The reconstruction was rededicated in 1720; the main church building having been rededicated at Easter in 1716. The building as we now know it was designed by James Gibbs with wood carving by Grinling Gibbons. The old Duke had his own pew in the West Gallery with seats at the entrance for his bodyguard.

The oldest buildings still remaining are the cottages with their overhanging first floors at the junction of Marsh Lane and Stanmore Broadway which are thought to have been built in the late 16th century and, as such, are protected by a preservation order. As they are all linked and have a common staircase to the upper floor their original use is the subject of much speculation. Was it an inn? Was it built for members of the same large family? Was it the parish almshouse? One legend suggests it was a home for lepers, whilst another that it was a refuge for Londoners escaping from the Great Plague.

Until the First World War Stanmore had its own brewery which supplied beer to the owning family's local public houses. The large lake on the opposite side of the road, now a reservoir attracting local fishermen, was once the parish's main water supply. As one descends the hill London's landmarks – although some ten miles distant – can be seen on a clear day, and it is noticeable that despite many modern buildings a number of the older properties have been retained and the Hill keeps its character.

At the bottom the Bernays Memorial Institute building (opened in 1870) met the social and religious needs of village life at the time and to a more limited extent does so today. It was built as a memorial to the son of the Reverend Bernays, rector of St John's from 1860–83, who was unfortunately drowned whilst on holiday.

Stanmore originally acquired its station in the late Victorian era when it was a terminus of the London and North Western Railway Company. At that time it occupied a great deal of land with sidings, depots and all the requisites of a terminus. This, of course, eventually became a terminus on the Bakerloo Line and is now serving the same purpose for the Jubilee Line.

Earl Attlee lived near the junction of Marsh Lane and The Broadway whilst Prime Minister. Since his time, and no doubt also before, this pleasant area has been the home of many stars of stage, screen and radio.

Stanwell

Stanwell village is now part of the borough of Spelthorne. It borders both the county of Buckinghamshire and the boroughs of Hounslow and Hillingdon. It is very close to Heathrow airport and indeed the cargo centre comes within the Stanwell boundary.

Rapid increase in population came about after the end of the Second World War. Prefabricated houses were built by Staines UDC to help satisfy the post-war need for housing. This was to be followed by a big estate of houses for airport employees. Before the Second World War the population was 3,275 and by the 1980s was over 9,000.

Stanwell land is mostly flat and part of Stanwell produces very good gravel. For these reasons it was chosen as the site of London airport and has been greatly sought after for its gravel. Sadly, it was to lose its manor house in the 1950s to a gravel company. This historic building was where Sir John Gibson, a world renowned engineer, lived and for this reason meetings were held in this house in connection with the Mulberry Harbour project during the Second World War.

Despite its growth there is still an atmosphere of a village. It has a centre with a village green, enjoying a backdrop of a most beautiful church. There are many flourishing associations. The Bowling Club is enjoying a very prosperous period. Although originally held in the vicarage garden it is now in the Recreation Ground. The Cricket Club is nigh on 150 years old.

Stanwell was written about in the Domesday Book (1086), which shows that there were four mills and that the land was held by Walter Fitzother, whose family name was to be changed to Windsor.

The two most historic buildings in the village are the parish church of St Mary and the Lord Knyvett School

133

Lord Knyvett School, Stanwell

building. The church dates in part from the 12th century. Its distinctive leaning spire was added in the 14th century and was caused to lean by the oak shingles drying out more quickly on one side. Services are held regularly and in 1988 a new organ was installed. In the churchyard is a tombstone with the date February 31st 1756 on it! There is also a Roman Catholic church dedicated to St David, a modern building of the late 1960s. In the southern part of the parish is a Congregational church in the heart of the residential area.

In the parish church is an effigy of Lord and Lady Knyvett above their tomb. It was sculpted by Nicholas Stone, the Royal Sculptor of the early 17th century, whose work can be seen in Westminster Abbey. Thomas, Lord Knyvett, was lord of the manor of Stanwell and an important member of the Court of Elizabeth I and James I. It was in his capacity as Chief Justice of the Peace for Westminster that he arrested Guy Fawkes. So highly valued were the Knyvetts by James I that he entrusted his two daughters to live with them in Stanwell 'to breathe the sweet air of Middlesex'. Lord Knyvett died in 1622 and in a codicil to his will he bequeathed money to build a school for the boys of the village. The school was opened in 1624 and continued in use until the 1960s. It was then used as an Adult Education Centre. It is a splendid Jacobean building. Monies for the youth of Stanwell is still available from Lord Knyvett's legacy, administered by a local management committee. Details of other charities, including one for elderly widows of the parish, can be seen on the board in the church.

Stanwell people campaigned for many years for a public library and a secondary school. Both were finally achieved but in recent cuts it was the Stanwell school that was axed. The library, although only open part of the week is greatly valued.

To look at Stanwell from the air it is obvious how much water there is, the predominant parts being the two reservoirs. The Staines reservoir (although in Stanwell) has a public path across it, not as is often thought because of its size, but because Stanwell people fought for this path to replace their walk from Stanwell to Staines. In the Second World War logs were floated in this reservoir to prevent German seaplanes from landing. The George VI reservoir was used as a decoy for London to confuse the enemy pilots, as it was lit from inside. The airmen responsible for this operation were billeted in the village and kept their secret to the end. Today the reservoirs are the rendezvous of many ornithologists.

Ashford hospital, once the site of the local workhouse, is situated within the Stanwell parish. The local health centre is named St David's and administered by a team of doctors and other medical personnel.

In the history of Stanwell it emerges quite clearly that there has always been great enthusiasm and energy exerted from the people to benefit the community. When the enclosure of Stanwell was proposed in the 1760s by the lord of the manor Stanwell people banded together, employed their own counsel and went to the Houses of Parliament in their farm carts. They won the day, that time. What a victory for the ordinary people!

Sudbury ✍

Sudbury today is a suburban area, much of it dating from between the two world wars. It was originally one of ten hamlets which formed the larger of the Archbishop of Canterbury's two Harrow manors and there are still parts which recall village life before the coming of the electric railway.

Little is known of the effect on the district of the Black Death of 1349, but it created a shortage of workers, and their wages rose somewhat. When things settled down again the landowners wished to revert to the old scale and this, plus a poll tax in 1377 and again in 1380 caused great frustration and resulted in the Peasants Revolt. Rebels in Middlesex had contact with Wat Tyler of Kent and serious disturbances occurred in the Sudbury/Harrow area. Sudbury was then an area of very large houses surrounded by land, and some small cottages occupied by agricultural labourers, drovers, shepherds and domestic servants.

In the 16th century Sudbury had some 20 to 30 households. The inhabitants of such a rural hamlet were not likely to trouble County Justices too much. Offences such as neglecting to clean ditches by the King's highway, or brewing and baking shortfalls and dilution were the main causes of complaints, resulting in fines (usually 2d) which sometimes were remitted because of poverty.

In the 17th century little had changed, but a more serious incident involved one William Page. The area is of London clay which made farming heavy and tried tempers. Two men had been sent to cart dung from Wealdstone across a common field to Sudbury and when William went to see how they were getting on he found the cart stuck fast, the horses unable to move it and the men preparing to return home with the horses leaving the cart. After a somewhat acrimonious argument, Mr Page seized the leading horse intending to put it back between the shafts. As he did so he threw away the billhook he was holding and by mischance struck one of the men on the back of his head, breaking his skull and causing his death.

Sudbury was an isolated hamlet and travel was hazardous. The enclosing of hundreds of acres turned the area into larger estates and less commonland, largely owned by the lord of the manor, Lord Northwick, who leased farms to substantial tenant farmers. Like the rest of southern England the Great Depression brought ruin to farmers. Thomas Anthony Trollope, father of the novelist, faced ruin despite vast reductions in his rent. He secretly conveyed his furniture to a friend for Mrs Trollope's benefit and sold the rest of his goods to raise £90 of the £220 he owed. He escaped arrest as a debtor by fleeing to Belgium and eventually the rest of the family followed him.

In 1841 the area was still largely agricultural. Of 117 non-domestic occupations recorded, 84 were agricultural, but village life was supported by shoemakers, wheelwrights, blacksmiths and carpenters. In 1844, a railway station opened one mile east of the hamlet and this began the spread of Sudbury over a wide area.

Aspen Lodge, at the junction of Sudbury Court Road, was a large house which became a college and was later taken over by Wembley Council for housing accommodation. In 1952, Egremont House on Sudbury Hill was seriously damaged by fire two months after an unsuccessful exorcism to rid the place of an energetic ghost! Sudbury Priory, built in 1828, was occupied by George Webster, a parliamentary agent. Barham Park mansion was the home of Sir Titus Barham, the man who began the Express Dairy, and had a model farm. 'The Chestnuts' on the Harrow Road was where Sir William Perkin lived. As an 18 year old he had experimented with a few chemicals trying to make quinine from a coal tar constituent called aniline. He instead isolated a dark substance which he found could dye silk a brilliant mauve. A craze for mauve developed and the initial successs of a factory built by William's father for providing the dye was assured. William retired and devoted himself to purely chemical research. The dye factory flourished until 1873, when an offer for the business was accepted.

In 1908, only 14 new houses existed in Rosebank Avenue where the Greenford Road runs. There were shops and a post office and a corrugated iron District railway station (now Sudbury Hill). The trains had shiny straw seats and were open at the ends with balconies, just like those seen on trains in old American movies. Waterlogged holes made by ruts from horses and carts made the lanes impassable in bad weather. This meant for children a journey to church and Sunday school passing a gipsy encampment and being harrassed by wild gangs, who would drag Sunday-clad victims behind the cottages and dump them in smelly pigswill!

Social life in the village revolved around the church. There was no wireless or picture house, until the great Empire Exhibition of 1924–25. The building of the stadium at Wembley brought crowds to the area, followed by developers and Sudbury village began to turn into a London suburb with rashes of red roofs.

Sunbury-on-Thames 🦢

Sunbury-on-Thames is one of the most southerly villages in the county of Middlesex, but is now administered by Surrey. Sunbury has many historical associations and celebrated the one thousandth anniversary of the signature of King Edgar's charter in 1962. The charter established that a Saxon lord, Sunna, had made his homestead near the river in the 10th century and that a man named Cruda had a ship building works on the Thames. There is still a boat builders on the Sunbury river frontage today, some sort of continuity having been preserved for over a millennium.

Although this may be the earliest recorded mention of Sunbury, there is evidence of earlier periods of occupation, the earliest of which was found on Sunbury common in 1870 – a cemetery of 72 inverted Middle Bronze Age burial urns containing cremated bones, which are now in the British Museum.

By the time of the Domesday Book, Sunbury was held by the Abbot of Westminster, and it was transferred to Queen Elizabeth I at sometime during her reign.

Kempton manor to the north passed to the Crown in 1217, possibly because the heir was a minor. Henry III built a royal hunting lodge which became a favourite royal residence until 1331, when it fell into disrepair. No trace has ever been found of this building, probably because in 1374 John of Kingston was given permission to sell all the timber and stone of Kempton manor house! However the park was used for hunting, especially in Tudor times when Henry VIII restocked the park with deer and Queen Elizabeth hunted from Hanworth. It was also on the route from Westminster to Windsor, so could well have been used as an overnight stopping place on the journey. One could say that there is still a royal connection as members of the royal family visit Kempton Park on racedays!

Probably the oldest building in Sunbury is the Three Fishes Inn at the bottom of Green Street. It has a timber frame which may be 16th century. Sunbury is noted for its many fine 17th and 18th century houses, though unfortunately many have been pulled down in recent years.

An interesting house in Lower Hampton Road is Darby House, named after Admiral George Darby. Some sources state that this house was designed by Sir Christopher Wren, but recent research seems to belie this. The south front of the house is the only example of Strawberry Hill Gothic architecture in Sunbury (influenced by Horace Walpole's home at Twickenham in the 18th century). Judge Jeffreys is said to have held court on this site in 1685, sentencing rebels after the battle of Sedgemoor.

Another admiral who lived in Sunbury was Admiral Lord Hawke who lived at Hawke House in Green Street from 1771 until his death in 1781. Hawke House is said to be haunted by the ghost of the Admiral, several owners and tenants having reported seeing it. Thomas Hughes, author of *Tom Brown's Schooldays* also lived there.

The Castle Inn, now a restaurant, has, on the second floor, a 'soldiers' room', a small uncomfortable room under the eaves which the inn had to provide to accommodate the military. A large upstairs room at the Flower Pot was probably used for Sunbury Manor Courts and for the Sunbury Petty Sessions, as well as for auctions. This room was declared unsafe in 1988, and amidst much local controversy was demolished by the brewers. The Flower Pot was a posting house for a while in the 19th century, and carried the tradition through to the 20th century when it was the site of Sunbury's first petrol filling station.

It is said that in the early years of the century trotting races were held on a Sunday from The Shears public house in Staines Road West to Sunbury Cross! Rumour has it that The Shears derived its name from the fact that local sheep were sheared nearby, and the actual shears used were in the possession of Mr Ballard of Vicarage Road, a Water Board 'turnkey'. He was a local character of great geniality and villagers always knew when the summer had arrived because Mr Ballard commenced wearing his straw boater!

Probably the largest and most impressive house in Sunbury is Sunbury Court, formerly Sunbury Place. The core of the house was built in the early years of the 18th century and it is marked on a map of 1754. It has had many additions and alterations but seems to have been well looked after. The Salvation Army bought the house in 1925 and it is now used as a conference centre. It has been restored recently and is a beautiful sight.

In the autumn of 1822 William Cobbett passed through Twickenham, Hampton, Sunbury and Shepperton and re-marked, acidly, 'The buildings consist generally of showy tea-garden-like boxes and of shabby dwellings of labouring people who are dirty and have every appearance of drinking gin'!

No trace has been found of an early church, nor of the Saxon church which is rumoured to have existed. The present church of St Mary was built in 1752. The old church had become so ruinous by 1750 that it was pulled down and the new church built on the same site. The old church probably dated from about the middle of the 14th century. The new church, designed by Stephen Wright, consisted of a tower and belfry and a rather plain, wide nave. The tower has a domed roof surmounted by a cupola. By 1870 Sunbury common was becoming well populated, so St Saviour's was built as a daughter church of St Mary's, becoming a separate parish in 1881.

There would appear to have been 'a little French church' in Sunbury in the early 18th century, built to serve the Huguenots who had settled here. By 1799 French Street was named after them and there are still some fine mulberry trees in and around the village which were planted at that time for the silk industry. The minister, Charles le Blanc, is said to have been there for 30 years before his death in 1735. No later references have been found.

By 1792 there were two Non-Conformist meeting houses in Sunbury. The present Congregational Church was built in 1903, replacing a series of chapels on various sites. The first Methodist Church was built in 1866 and replaced a coach house which had been used before. The present church and halls were commenced in 1957 and gradually took over the work of the old building, which was demolished. There is a meeting place for the Plymouth Brethren in Burgoyne Road and a Lutheran Church in Groveley Road.

In about 1830 the Assembly Rooms in Thames Street were built. In 1895 they were used for a while for Council meetings (Sunbury U.D.C. having been formed in 1894), but by the 1920s they had been converted into a cinema and later became part of an engineering works; this is where the 'ticker tape' was manufactured during the War to foil the German radar. Recently the Assembly Rooms have been taken over as the Riverside Arts Centre.

Sunbury was almost the furthest upstream of the towns and villages on the Thames which became popular with the upper and middle classes. It never became fashionable like Richmond, Twickenham or Hampton, nonetheless a number of famous people are reputed to have lived in Sunbury. A fine Tudor mansion, on the site of Ivy House in French Street, was once the home of Thomas Cromwell when he was administering the building of Hampton Court, and the Earl of Essex is said to have lived there. Anthony Trollope, the 19th century author lived and went to school in Sunbury, and Edward, Prince of Wales was a frequent visitor to Monksbridge in Thames Street during the 1930s. Contemporary famous residents have included Alma Cogan, Adam Faith and Tom Jones.

The land around Sunbury appears to have been farmed on the open-field plan until enclosure in 1803, when much of the land was used for market gardening. The River Gardens estate, completed – or rather not fully completed – just before the outbreak of the Second World War was situated on old orchards reputed to belong to Pouparts, jam manufacturers, so most of the houses had one or two fruit trees in the gardens, some of which still exist today. A large common meandered across open country towards Hanworth. Even in the early days of the war it was delightful to picnic there with the children and come home with a bunch of cowslips.

The main highway from Kingston to Staines ran over Sunbury common (as it does today) and was said to be in a dreadful state for most of the year, and there was the added hazard of thieves on the lonely stretches of the common. In 1789 John Bunce of Teddington was robbed of his silver watch and seven and a half guineas in gold as he returned home across Sunbury common.

Gradually, after the coming of the railway, Sunbury common, or Upper Sunbury, began to be developed. The earliest of the factories appeared and with the Metropolitan Water Board reservoirs and waterworks needing workers, housing was built mainly along the Staines Road and Vicarage Road. Some of the houses in Vicarage Road (now much altered internally) are said to be built from materials salvaged from alterations at Hampton Court Palace. Certainly the staircases went straight up from front doors at the side and were separated from the rooms to either side by old doors and planking.

One of the more interesting of the industries at Sunbury Cross is that of board making. Mr Daniel Sutherland came to Sunbury in the 1880s and invented woodfibre board, later hardboard, in 1898. The company is still producing a quality board known as 'Sundeala Medium' on the same site as it was nearly 100 years ago.

One of the famous landmarks in Spelthorne is Sunbury Clock, which was erected at the junction of the six crossroads at Sunbury Cross in 1897 to celebrate Queen Victoria's Diamond Jubilee. This became a very busy junction and it was badly damaged by a lorry in 1966. It now stands outside the parade of shops on Staines Road West.

Another feature which is well known locally is the Lendy Lion. This was originally a memorial fountain erected in 1895 on Church Wharf, surmounted by the lion, in memory of two brothers named Lendy who died, one in Bulawayo and one on the West Coast of Africa, in 1894. The fountain was destroyed by a bomb in the Second World War and the lion was kept in the grounds of the council offices at Benwell House. The lion now has pride of place in the walled gardens on the edge of Sunbury Park opposite the Magpie. Incidentally, the Magpie was the original meeting place of the Grand Order of Water Rats, and there is a plaque on the wall outside to commemorate the event.

The river is an important part of Sunbury and parts of the bank and Rivermead Island are valuable open spaces. A popular feature every summer is Sunbury Regatta, the first of which took place in 1877 and a firework display was first introduced in 1880. It is interesting to note that gravel digging was first recorded as early as 1636 when certain individuals were given the right to dredge the river bottom for gravel. Most of the open space around Sunbury has been dug for gravel, but the companies always seem to be looking for more to keep pace with modern building!

Perhaps the most colourful ceremony which can be seen in Sunbury is the 500 year old custom of Swan Upping. A procession of small boats leaves Turk's Boatyard in the third week of July, managed by Mr John Turk, the Queen's Swanmaster. The swan is a royal bird and two thirds of the population belong to the Crown and so have Royal protection. The rest belong either to the Company of Vintners or the Company of Dyers. The purpose of this ceremony is to mark the cygnets with the same mark as that of their parents so that ownership can be established.

Teddington 🪶

Prehistoric remains have been found in the Teddington area; a barrow just off Sandy Lane was excavated during the 19th century and found to contain several disturbed burials. There were some flint tools and part of a bronze dagger.

Up to the middle of the 19th century the area was sparsely populated, mainly by farmers, fishermen, basket weavers and those in service on the large estates. In the 1860s there was a sudden increase in the population, which almost quadrupled in ten years. This was mainly due to the coming of the railway and the breaking up of the manor.

One of the oldest houses in Teddington was Queen Elizabeth's Hunting Lodge which dated from 1564. This house is reputed to have been used by guests from Hampton Court. There is a letter from the Earl of Leicester to Queen Elizabeth dated in 1570 which was addressed from Teddington. The house was demolished in 1875.

Many famous people have lived in Teddington including John Walter, who founded *The Times* – supposedly to keep his printing machine busy. R. D. Blackmore, the author of *Lorna Doone*, taught Classics at Hampton Grammar School for a while, a job he never liked, and had a house and garden in Teddington for more than 40 years. Many of his fruit trees are said to be bearing fruit in gardens in the town. Stephen Hales was vicar of Teddington from about 1709 to 1761 and was one of those 18th century parsons who were also eminent scientists. Apart from being an active parish priest, he enlarged the church and churchyard and provided the village with a clean and plentiful water supply. He wrote a book on 'Vegetable Staticks', his researches for which advanced considerably the knowledge of the anatomy of plants. He invented a ventilating machine which was a hand-operated type of organ bellows which freshened the air in confined spaces and which was applied with good effect in slave ships, naval ships and prisons. Apparently it reduced mortality in Newgate Prison by half and practically banished gaol fever.

One of the best remembered old time residents was Peg Woffington. She had a short but brilliant London stage career – she played Polly in John Gay's *The Beggars' Opera* – retiring in 1757. She is said to have given the cottages bearing her name to the poor, but there seems little evidence to connect her with them. They bear the date 1759 but contain work of an earlier time. She died in 1760 at the age of 39 and the cottages are now used as a tea room and restaurant.

Teddington Dairy in Vicarage Road had an interesting history. From 1819 onwards villagers were served with dairy produce by 'cow-keepers' who kept their herds in fields surrounding the High Street. In 1874 two enterprising country girls, Louisa and Sally Barber, came to Teddington and married Mr Roberts and Mr Prewett respectively and set about improving the dairy business. By 1899 Louisa had married her second husband, Mr Job. The Roberts family founded the Coombe Bakeries, Prewett's Dairies were in business up until a few years ago and Job's grew into a very large concern based at Hanworth and Didcot. It was only sold out to Unigate in the 1980s and Job's lorries and milk floats are still to be seen in the area.

There was 'the largest and most complete' wax and candle factory in Waldegrave Road during the 18th, 19th and early 20th centuries. The finest white wax was made and then bleached in the fields. The product was so good that it was

146

even sold to the Vatican. Nearly four acres were said to be covered with wax in summer and 200,000 lbs were bleached each year. The premises were taken over by the Paint Research Association in 1927.

There would seem to have been many wealthy residents in the 19th century and at the beginning of the 20th. Many shops were built, at least five new churches, a public library and an opulent town hall, which contained a theatre and a ballroom. The town hall was burnt down in 1903 and never rebuilt as it had not been a financial success.

In 1832 a public school was opened for 60 boys. Funds were obtained by public subscription and a house was built for the master. A further school was opened in 1843 for girls and infants. Money was also raised for a cottage hospital in Elfin Grove in 1875 and this became rather dilapidated after the First World War. A series of fetes were held to raise money for a new hospital and the first part of the War Memorial Hospital was opened in 1929.

St Alban's church was built in 1887 and opened in 1889. The public subscription raised more money than was expected. The plan was for a large building almost on the scale of a Gothic cathedral, and with the extra money stone was substituted for a lot of the brick. It was quite a landmark with its gleaming copper roof. However it was never completed and some years ago it was declared redundant and the parish was handed back to St Mary's.

There is about two miles of river frontage so the Thames is important to Teddington. Teddington Lock is the dividing line between the Port of London Authority and the Thames Conservancy, and many people will have heard of Teddington in that the flow of the Thames is very precisely monitored and recorded at Teddington Weir.

Bushy House and Park are very much part of Teddington although the park stretches to Hampton. Bushy Park was enclosed from part of Hounslow Heath in stages from the

15th to the 17th centuries. The park was set out in its present form by Henry Wise in co-operation with Christopher Wren on the orders of William III. Wren envisaged it as a triumphal way to his new north front of Hampton Court Palace, which he designed but which was never built.

In Victorian and Edwardian times Londoners used to visit Bushy Park on Chestnut Sunday (that nearest to 11th May) and picnic under the flowering trees. From 1874 to 1882 the park became the venue of cycling clubs. In 1882 183 cycling clubs took part and the meeting had become too big and was abandoned. Today Bushy Park is enjoyed by walkers, horse riders and paddle boaters on the old fish pond. There is an interesting and adventurous children's playground and there is still a herd of deer. The gate to Bushy House from the park used to be guarded by two cannon probably dating from the Crimean campaign. They were removed for scrap in the Second World War. However the gate is still known as Cannon Gate.

Bushy House was originally the Middle Lodge of the park. There were two lodges which were normally lived in by the Park Rangers. The office of Ranger seems to have become a ploy for the Sovereign to give tenancy of the house.

Prince William Henry, Duke of Clarence, third son of George III, lived almost half his life in Bushy House. Dorothy Jordan was an actress who made her stage debut in 1785 and by 1791 she and the Duke were to all intents and purposes man and wife. They were not allowed to marry by reason of the Royal Marriage Act. In 1797 the Duke of Clarence was given the Rangership. He and Mrs Jordan had three children by then and a further seven Fitzclarence children were born in Bushy House. The Duke of Clarence lived the life of a country squire for many years, but in 1811, for reasons which are not clear, Mrs Jordan moved out and died about five years later.

In 1900 Queen Victoria exchanged the house for some

148

Government property in Pall Mall. The National Physical Laboratory moved in in 1902, using the kitchen for experimental work. Further land was acquired in 1921 and many purpose-built laboratories erected. Today the House is occupied by the Director of the National Physical Laboratory and the NPL has been joined by the Admiralty Research Laboratory, British Calibration Society, National Weights and Measures Laboratory and in 1988, the Laboratory of the Government Chemist. In spite of all the building that has gone on, a public right of way to the park was preserved by constructing part of one of the NPL buildings over the footpath.

Teddington today is a busy place and densely populated though it still retains features of the old village. It has many thriving societies and sports facilities, many involving the river. The government laboratories and the television studios as well as the many offices are the largest employers.

Twickenham ఆ

The old village of Twickenham developed on the northern branch of the Thames, on a delightful stretch of the river. Its strategic position on the way up to Hampton Court led to the establishment of country houses for the rich merchants and noblemen. There was a good livelihood for innkeepers and shopkeepers to serve these houses and on the river for osiers, bargemen and ferrymen.

A short lane still slopes from Twickenham High Street to the river leading to a pretty hoop-shaped bridge over to Eel Pie Island. Until the building of this footbridge in 1957, contact was by ferry. It used to be a favourite spot for anglers and boating parties and was named after one of the dishes served at Eel Pie House in the 18th century. It is now a kind of miniature bungalow town and the whole island is only two acres in extent.

On the mainland is the Riverside Inn. This was a boys school from the 15th century until 1727, when it was turned into a tavern. It is still a port of call for the Swan Uppers on their annual trip up the Thames.

Beyond the pub is a high wall curving round the churchyard of St Mary the Virgin. A seven and a half ft high mark shows the level to which the Thames flooded in March 1774. Of the original 15th century parish church only the stone tower remains. The body of the church was rebuilt in warm red brick in 1714–15. Many famous 18th century people who lived in Twickenham attended services here, including Alexander Pope (who is buried in a vault under the middle aisle), Horace Walpole, the painter Kneller and Kitty Clive, one of the cleverest of 18th century comediennes.

There is another church in Twickenham, All Hallows on the Chertsey Road. It was only put up at the beginning of the 1940s to serve the new housing estates developed on the old nurseryland and orchards, but history was built into it. The ancient church of All Hallows in the City of London was one of the redundant churches scheduled for demolition. The tower by Sir Christopher Wren was dismantled stone by stone, brought to the site in Chertsey Road and carefully re-erected. The old altar, pulpit and choir stalls were also brought to beautify the new church, together with some of the memorial tablets.

Most of the streets in the old part of Twickenham have long been rebuilt, but one which retains its characteristics is Church Street. Once part of the old Bath Road, most of the buildings have been restored and are attractive little shops. The corner shop, No 54, is said to have been built by Samuel Mesley (1792–1868), bootmaker and the last beadle of Twickenham, and the name can be seen over the door.

Terraces of houses were a feature of 18th and early 19th century architecture and Montpelier Row and Sion Row are fine examples surviving in Twickenham. Lord Tennyson and

Walter de la Mare were for a time residents in Montpelier Row.

Of all the fine riverside houses in Twickenham, the most famous is paradoxically no longer in sight of the Thames. When Horace Walpole bought a cottage in 1747 and spent 30 years converting it into the fine Gothic style battlemented castle called Strawberry Hill, he could sit and watch the barges from his windows. Now there is a barrier of high trees and rows of houses between his mansion and the river. Today Strawberry Hill is St Mary's Training College for teachers, but in appearance it is still the 18th century vision of the Gothic with its arched windows, fretwork screens, stained glass and gold-patterned fan-vaulting.

York House is a handsome example of a late 17th century mansion which was in the possession of the Crown. It was given by Charles II to his brother James, Duke of York. James and his wife lived for a time at York House and the future Queen Anne was born there. In 1924 York House was sold to Twickenham Urban Council and became their headquarters. In 1965 it became the home of the new London Borough of Richmond upon Thames.

Along the river from York House and up a flight of wooden steps, out of reach of the once-flooding Thames, is an old inn built in 1640, the White Swan, a favourite place for Thames bargemen in the past. Beyond the Swan is the entrance to the grounds of Orleans House. The original house built in 1709 has been demolished but the Octagon Room was purchased by the Hon Mrs Nellie Ionides, who left the room and a collection of 18th and 19th century pictures and local topographical drawings to the Borough of Twickenham. A gallery was built incorporating the Octagon and exhibitions and concerts are held there.

A few minutes walk along the towpath is Marble Hill House and Park. This Palladian villa was built in the early 18th century by Henrietta Howard, later the Countess of

Suffolk, with money secretly given her by George III, whose 'exceedingly respectable and respected mistress' she had been for years. Alexander Pope was her neighbour. His villa was pulled down at the beginning of the 19th century but Marble Hill is little changed today. In the gardens are dark ilex trees, a rare black walnut and the tallest Lombardy poplar in Britain. Another huge tree, said to be the biggest weeping willow in the country grows in nearby Radnor Gardens, where the Earl of Radnor had a mansion which was destroyed by a high explosive bomb in 1940.

In the Whitton area of Twickenham lies Kneller Hall. The original house was built in 1709–11 and was the home of the Court painter, Sir Godfrey Kneller. The house was virtually rebuilt and given a new front and became the Royal Military School of Music in 1857, where musicians for the army are trained. A concert in the outdoor arena which includes Tchaikovsky's 1812 Overture with accompanying cannon and firework display is a real experience!

In the mid 18th century the 3rd Duke of Argyll laid out his estate at Whitton Park with fine ornamental lake, Gothic tower and cedar trees. Despite attempts to preserve part for public use virtually all the original park was built over by 1934.

To many people in the country, Twickenham means only one thing – rugby. The Rugby Football Union decided in 1907 to have its own ground and purchased just over ten acres in Twickenham. The man behind the scheme was Billy Williams, Middlesex wicket keeper and bowler and well known rugby referee. In the early days the new ground was known as 'Billy Williams' cabbage patch' because the land had previously been used for allotments. In fact the rugby ground was surrounded by nurseries and orchards until the extensive housing developments of the 1930s. The RFU now has over 30 acres including large car parks.

Today Twickenham has little in the way of industry but

has a number of office blocks and a film studio in The Barons. It is largely a commuter area for central London and for Richmond upon Thames and Kingston upon Thames.

Uxbridge ✤

Uxbridge was originally a hamlet in the parish of Hillingdon, and is not mentioned in the Domesday Book, although it was almost certainly in existence before 1086 and had a market charter from 1180.

St Margaret's church was originally a chapel of ease to St John the Baptist's church in Hillingdon and the present building dates partly from the 14th and 15th centuries. The 15th century hammerbeam roof is thought to be one of the best of its kind in Middlesex. There was no burial ground in Uxbridge until the 16th century, all those who died having to be carried to Hillingdon to be buried. Then a plot of land at the bottom of Windsor Street was given to the village by Henry, Earl of Derby.

To the left of the church in Windsor Street are several small shops, some of which are very old, and most of the street is listed as worthy of preservation. The Queen's Head pub dates back to about 1540 and there is an ancient lamp outside the police station. At the bottom of Windsor Street lies the Old Burial Ground. The covered archway beside the Three Tuns – a 16th century posting house – leads into a yard, where horses used to be stabled. These yards are a feature of Uxbridge High Street, and they were the homes of the poor until the beginning of this century.

The Crown and Treaty House is Elizabethan, built of brick and with tall chimneys. This got its name in 1645, when an attempt was made to end the Civil War, and Royalist and Parliamentary representatives, quartered in lodgings on opposite sides of the High Street, met here to try to reach an

Windsor Street, Uxbridge

agreement. They failed and no treaty was signed. Parliamentary troops were stationed in Uxbridge, where the Non-Conformist population would have supported their cause.

The modern town of Uxbridge is the administrative centre of the London Borough of Hillingdon. It has a magistrates court, a county court, industrial estates and the Brunel University campus. There are multiple stores and supermarkets in traffic-free pedestrian precincts. The market place, now called 'The Pavilions', is designed for beautiful stalls and a feature tower soars to the high point of the glazed roof. The special glass of the roof maintains a light, bright summery feel all year round.

The RAF station at Uxbridge, one of the oldest in the Royal Air Force, is the headquarters of the RAF School of Music, the RAF Central Band, and HM the Queen's Colour Squadron. The underground control room is preserved, from which the defence of London and the South-east of England was controlled during the Battle of Britain in 1940.

Recreational facilities include the modern Beck theatre at Hayes, a golf course, cricket club, open air swimming pool, a manmade ski slope, and Fassnidge Park.

Wealdstone 🌿

In 1754 John Rocque, land surveyor, published a 'New and Accurate Map of the Country adjacent to the Cities'. His purpose was that 'it is universally allowed that such a map will be of great use to all Directors of Insurance Offices and Commissioners of Turnpikes, to Church Wardens and Overseers, to all Persons who have Occasions to travel, for Business, Health or Pleasure, and lastly to all curious Persons at Home or Abroad.' Rocque's map shows the Weald Stone, believed to indicate the boundary between the Weald (an area of dense woodland spread across the north of Middlesex) and the parish of Harrow. Nearby was Wealdstone House and Wealdstone Farm.

In 1834 the sunken stone came to light when the foundations of the Red Lion were put in. A newer building was later built further back and the Weald Stone is now visible at the foot of the sign, much nearer to the road. However, this is in Harrow Weald, not Wealdstone.

When the London to Birmingham Railway Company projected its line through Harrow, local opposition deflected its route away from Harrow Hill. The site finally chosen was alongside the ancient Harrow Lane, and a collection of 'mediocre houses and shops' sprang up, taking the name of Wealdstone. The station was first called 'Harrow Station', then 'Station End' (as in Station End Chapel). Nowadays it is 'Harrow and Wealdstone', having been rebuilt in 1923.

In July 1837 the new railway attracted many visitors and it is recorded that beer from the Queen's Arms was ladled out in pails in the street! In 1846 the London Birmingham

155

Railway Company amalgamated with others to form the London and North Western Railway Company.

With the railway established, there followed the expansion of homes and factories. In 1854 the City of London and Counties Freehold Land Society proposed a 'Harrow Park Estate', which named Canning Road, Peel Road and Palmerston Road. Plots for shops along Station Road (High Street) were priced from £40. However, by 1863 Palmerston Road was still a muddy lane of small farms. In 1892 Wealdstone Ratepayers Defence Association was demanding 'Home Rule for Wealdstone' and two years later came the setting up of Wealdstone Urban District Council. From then on the name was well and truly recognised.

Wealdstone remained a compact area with shops, church, pubs and police station along the High Street and just a few shops on and over the railway bridge and down Mason's Avenue. The surrounding area remained rural with many springs in the clay soil forming brooks and streams.

In 1890 Kodak purchased seven acres of land to establish their first factory. By 1965 the factory had 55 acres with 100 buildings and was employing 5,500 people.

Hamilton's brush works were established in 1897. Printing works, gun making, a coffin factory, Winsor & Newton and, by 1923, Whitefriars glass works all created local employment.

An early photograph shows the local fire brigade, a voluntary body consisting of two horses, an engine and eleven men. The carriage building workshops of J. Knott (later Winfield's, ironmonger) was the first designated fire station, with an illuminated sign outside. Opposite, outside Holy Trinity church, a fire bell was suspended from the top of a wooden post and set ringing by a hanging rope. Bob Harwood and Ted Daniels used their two horses with the council's tip-up refuse carts. It is said that, when the fire bell was heard, unhitched *Bob* and *Nancy* would recognise the alarm and make their own way to the fire station, with their owners often chasing after them! Among the brigade's equipment, hay cutting knives are listed, for haystacks often caught fire, burning from inside, and had to be cut apart in order to quench the fire.

Later the Kodak hooter gave the alarm. This always sounded for the workers at 7 am and 1 pm with a short blast five minutes later. Three blasts indicated a local fire, six short blasts a Kodak fire. The works have always had their own fire brigade and, during the First World War, it was often called to fires in London. Wealdstone had its first motor fire engine in 1924 and, by the Second World War, was part of the National Fire Service. Nowadays the nearest fire station is in Wembley.

Wealdstone brook and other streams were fed by many springs in the clay soil. These gave rise to flooding and the formation of many ponds – useful for horses and cattle and an entertainment for children. Eventually, by the 1970s, the streams were culverted. Occasionally the drains cannot cope with a sudden heavy downpour and, as in the old days, Wealdstone High Street will be flooded.

Wembley 🌿

The old village of Wembley, only seven miles from Marble Arch, was part of Harrow. It was given to the Priory of Kilburn, in the 13th century and to Richard Page after the Dissolution of the Monasteries. In 1810 the manor house at Wembley Park was rebuilt by the Gray family.

Little now remains of that historical past. The estate was bought by the Metropolitan Railway Company, who built a line through part of the grounds and sold the rest in 1890 to a company who planned to create a pleasure park. Sir Edward Watkin was to build a tower to reach the height of 1200 ft, to rival the Eiffel Tower in Paris, but funds ran out and the tower only reached the first storey, later to be demolished.

In 1920 Wembley was still just a dot on the map, but in 1922 work began on the building of Wembley Stadium for the proposed British Empire Exhibition and things began to change. The Stadium was ready for use by April 1923 and the FA Cup Tie was played there between Bolton Wanderers and West Ham United. In 1924 the Empire Exhibition was opened by King George V and Queen Mary, displaying exhibits from all the countries of the Empire, its trades and its peoples.

Thousands of people flocked to Wembley and big business in the form of development came with them. Trams ran through the High Road, linking Sudbury with Paddington, and there were pirate buses, run by private companies eager to cash in on the boom. Later most of the Exhibition buildings were taken over as factories.

The council offices were in the High Road, and where British Home Stores now stands was the fire station, with a single ambulance based in St John's Road. Refuse collection was done by horse-drawn vans of a singular shape, the stables being in Eccleston Mews. There were several contractors with horse carts which could be hired.

The railway service was quite good, but some of the stations, including Alperton, have since been moved from their original positions. By 1934 when the Empire Pool was built, Wembley was a very big and thriving place. The volume of traffic had increased so much that road improvements became essential and involved the straightening and widening of North Wembley railway bridge. The building of many new houses in the locality made more stations necessary, eg South Kenton. The milkman changed his way of life and no longer was milk sold straight from a churn, direct to the jug at the door. Instead milk in bottles arrived on an electrically motivated trolley, and his horse was pensioned off to stables in Brook Avenue.

Wembley was now 'on the map' and was granted its Borough Charter in 1937, the first mayor nominated being Sir Titus Barham, whose father founded Express Dairies and who resided in a large mansion in Barham Park. At the mayoral inauguration Sir Titus was to have ridden horseback through many of the streets of Wembley, but unfortunately he died on that very day.

A new town hall, called by Pevsner 'the best of the modern town halls around London, neither fanciful nor drab', was built in the late 1930s in Forty Avenue. Came the Second World War, and Wembley had its share of trouble from enemy action. Refugees from Europe were housed in the Empire Pool.

Wembley was proud to be the base for the Olympic Games staged in England in 1948, from 29th July to 14th August. The Stadium and Pool were the scene for many events and the marathon race took place almost entirely in Middlesex. Runners went along the Barnet by-pass to Stirling Corner in Hertfordshire, carried on a little further north, then went west across to Watling Street and so southwards back to the Stadium. Perhaps the greatest performance in the Olympics of that year was by the Dutch woman athlete, who won the 80 metres, 100 metres and 200 metres, Fanny Blankers-Koen.

During the reorganisation of London boroughs, Wembley and Willesden were joined to become the Greater London Borough of Brent. The FA Cup Final is now only one big day in the year at the Stadium. Many other events take place there, including vast open air pop concerts, and with the wind in the right – or wrong – direction, they can be heard as far away as Alperton!

West Drayton 🖗

A village steeped in history but now more a suburban area, West Drayton is one of the few Middlesex villages to have retained its village green with many interesting buildings. In the 19th century the green boasted five public houses, now reduced to one.

The Women's Institute hall, also on the green, has been adapted to provide a medical centre for local doctors. Still existing on the green is the mid 18th century building which was the village general store. In 1766 the shop was bought by John Haynes. He paid £26.0s.10¼d for the stock and fittings and the property remained in the ownership of the family for the following 200 years. A descendant Dudley Haynes was a well known artist in the 1920s and 1930s and exhibited at the Royal Academy.

Southlands, an early Georgian house at the south end of the green, is now a flourishing local arts centre. Among the people who lived there in the past were the author Cosmo Hamilton and his actress wife Beryl Faber who was the sister of the famous actor Sir Aubrey Smith. Sir Aubrey, who captained England in a Test Match in 1888, also lived in West Drayton from the early part of the century. He became a member of the local cricket club in 1902 and retained his interest in the village throughout his life.

One of the oldest houses in the village is now a National Trust property and known as St George's Meadows. It was originally a Tudor farmhouse. The author Havelock Ellis lived there for some years before the First World War.

Beyond the green on the river Colne there has been a mill since the time of the Domesday Book. It operated as a board and paper mill in the 19th century but was burned down in 1913. The Mill House is a fine example of Georgian architecture and was for a time the home of Sir Allen Lane who founded Penguin Books.

M. Evans.

West Drayton Green

The parish church of St Martin dates from the 13th century on the site of a former Norman church. It was rebuilt in the 15th century incorporating part of the earlier structure. The crypt contains the coffins of the Paget and De Burgh families from the 16th to the 19th centuries and according to legend is haunted by a raven.

Next to the church stands the Gatehouse, the only surviving part of the manor house built by Sir William Paget about 1550. In 1591 the house was leased to Lord Hunsdon who entertained Queen Elizabeth I there in 1602. The house was demolished about 1750 but the Gatehouse remained a private residence, used as the vicarage in the 19th century.

Winchmore Hill ✤

Eight miles from the Bank of England but only one mile from Hertfordshire and the Green Belt, it is thought to derive its name from the whin or furze bushes which flourished on the moor on the hill. By easy transition the name became Wynchmoor and so to Winchmore Hill. It was part of the great Forest of Middlesex and a few great oaks and chestnuts remain. It was a royal hunting forest and names such as Houndsden Road, Chase Side, Fox Lane and Old Park Ridings still indicate their ancient use.

In the time of James I, an old woman, Elizabeth Sawyer, was put on trial for being a witch. She had only one eye and was found to have a black mark on her back which apparently proved that she was in league with the Devil, so she was convicted!

There has always been a village green here and although it is smaller than of yore it is the centre of the village. A horse trough is still on one side but an old fountain disappeared not long ago. The village pump and well used to be here for the use of all the inhabitants. Up to 100 years ago the village fair was looked forward to by everybody and became so popular that it continued for three days, but finally there was not enough room so it moved to a larger ground. Shops surround the green but the old bakery has now become an antique shop and several more jewellery, china and furniture antique shops now offer their wares.

In the 17th century when Quakers were being persecuted and it was a criminal offence to attend any other place of worship than the Church of England, a few of them found the quiet hamlet of Winchmore Hill and settled here. Later they built the Friends Meeting House in Church Hill which has the date 1688 over the door. It is a plain structure with its own large and beautiful garden burial ground. George

Fox was a frequent visitor and preached here. There are the graves of many well-known Quakers including members of the Barclay and Hoare families of bankers. In 1823 Elizabeth Fry recorded in her diary that she had attended Winchmore Hill meeting with her brother Samuel.

In 1828 Winchmore Hill had 50 houses and its quiet character induced Tom Hood, the prince of humorists and maker of puns, to make his home in Vicars Moor Lane. He came to Rose Cottage with his bride Jane Reynolds and his second daughter was born there in 1830. He wrote an amusing description of Winchmore Hill in verse called *Our Village* in which he mentions a pound and bowling and cricket taking place on the green. Alas, a German bomb in 1941 landed squarely on the cottage demolishing it completely. All that remains is an old brick wall and a blue plaque on the side of a modern house commemorating Rose Cottage and its owner.

The families of the Taylors and the Walkers (brewers) were the big local landowners. In 1882, Mr Mann of the firm of brewers Mann Crossman and Paulin also lived in Winchmore Hill and his son, Sir Edward Mann lived in Vicars Moor Lane. Miss Paulin was a great benefactress to the village and gave the land for the Winchmore Hill Cricket Club.

The Walkers lived in Southgate and with their nine sons often played cricket against the Taylors of Grovelands. Mr Taylor bought up as much land as he could and pulled down cottages and houses as he said that he could not bear to see other people's chimneys from his house! His land finally extended from Southgate Circus, through Winchmore Hill Road, Church Hill to the Bourne. His house, Grovelands, was built by John Nash in 1797 and is a Grade I listed building. Of classical design, the ground floor windows are surmounted by fan-fluted tympana set between giant Ionic pilasters and columns. It is surrounded by a ha-ha, made to

The Salisbury Arms &
old Butchers shop.

Salisbury Arms at Winchmore Hill

keep out the herd of red deer in the park at the time. Mr Taylor had a large lake made with an island in the centre which is a great attraction now, as in 1902 the estate was sold and later the District Council bought 91 acres for a public park.

Mr Taylor fought hard against the coming of the railway on his land but progress had its way. Palmers Green Station was built and the line extended through Winchmore Hill and Grange Park to Enfield. This took a slice from his land, mainly through the woods up to the bridge in Hoppers Road, known as the 'skew' bridge. Earlier this century there was only a path through these woods leading from the village green to Bourne Hill, where there was a keeper's cottage and the Woodman Inn which is still there. In the 1920s a wide road was made here and some of the finest houses were built.

In 1916 Captain Taylor lent the house as a hospital. In 1921 it was purchased by the Middlesex VAD and given to the Royal Northern Hospital as a convalescent home. It fell into disrepair but now it is being restored and will be a psychiatric hospital. Groveland Park is a great asset to the neighbourhood. It contains a nine hole pitch and putt golf course, football fields, tennis courts, a children's playground and an excellent bowling green.

Two other mansions were to be found until fairly recently in Winchmore Hill. Stone Hall in Church Hill was so called as it was built from stones moved from Old Blackfriars Bridge. The Regnart family who owned the original Maples, the furniture shop in Tottenham Court Road lived here. Mr Horace Regnart wrote a book about Winchmore Hill and its occupants and he is remembered striding about the village with his stick and deerstalker hat and wearing his monocle. His sister used to drive around in a pony carriage. When the land was sold and the house pulled down, the stones made the foundation for a new road now called Stonehall Road.

Another big house, Eversley, has suffered the same fate

and houses now in Green Dragon Lane and Eversley Park Road were built on this estate. The Lodge for Eversley Park still stands on the corner of Eversley Crescent and Green Dragon Lane. There were many fine trees in the gardens of this house and the Scots pines which border the roads and the old cedar were no doubt in the estate when the Marchioness of Ely lived here.

Winchmore Hill Cricket Club has played on its present ground for many years. Miss Paulin owned the land and on her death in 1960 left the land to the club for 99 years at a rent of one shilling per year. The club promptly paid 99 shillings and began to improve the facilities. During the Second World War, when people did not have petrol to go far afield, the cricket was quite an attraction. One day in summer the field was surrounded three deep with spectators as a match was played against the West Indies.

The village is fortunate in having two golf courses adjacent, as well as so much open space as London grows and encroaches on its environment up to the Green Belt.

Yeading

Yeading was mentioned in documents as early as AD 757, a hamlet in the parish of Hayes.

The population at the end of the 19th century was about 2,600. There were four main farms – Yeading Green Farm, Yeading Hall Farm, Poplar Farm (rumour has it that Oliver Cromwell stayed here) and Manor Farm, which dated back to 1307. A Mr Liddell who lived here was a magistrate and used to buy the boys and girls of the village boots and jerseys at Christmas.

One of the two cottages at Yeading Lane corner was a coffee stall called Hall's Halt. It was a good pull up for car men when there were horses and carts on the roads.

There was an isolation hospital at Yeading. A family named Hunt lived in a train converted into a house.

The first school was closed in 1861, when the masters and mistresses transferred to the Biscoe School at Norwood. There was a Yeading National School in 1903 and the Church of England school opened in 1904, but closed in 1924.

The next school was opened in 1906 and in 1910 it had 20 pupils. Miss Elsie Kitson was one of the first teachers at Yeading. The Yeading Infants School in Carlyon Road celebrates its 50th Anniversary in 1989.

Thomas Clayton owned the brickworks at Yeading and Clayton Cottages were named after him. When the brickworks finished the area became a huge rubbish tip and enormous barges brought glass and rubbish from the blitz in London during the Second World War. The last barges came down in 1948.

There were no churches in the area until 1902, although there has long been a Mission Hall at the corner of Yeading Fork and Willow Tree Lane. The Apostolic Church registered this chapel in 1954. In 1961 the church of St Edmund of Canterbury was consecrated.

Yeading Bridge is reported to have existed since 1825. Yeading Brook, which runs into the river Crane, was called Fiscebourne in AD 757 and was known for its salmon. There were net makers here at this time.

Melior Cottages in Yeading Lane were built in the 1920s, the first council houses in the area. They have been completely remodernised and many tenants have bought their properties. In 1949 there was a big development at Barnhill. Many roads were named after well known Labour people, Kier Hardie, Attlee, Morrison, etc. In 1960 there was a development around Perth Avenue and Dunedin Way.

There were munition works here during the Second World War and a block-house still exists. During and after the war there was an influx of people from the East End of London.

It was said that in the early days people who lived in Yeading had a certain way of speaking. In the early 19th century it was observed that at Yeading 'dirt, ignorance and darkness' reigned supreme but happily in 1874 the inhabitants of Yeading were 'always found civil'!

Today there are shops at Yeading and the new by-pass is awaited with eagerness to relieve the terrible traffic congestion in Yeading Lane.

Yiewsley

Yiewsley is on the extreme western edge of the county of Middlesex. The derivation of the name is obscure. The hamlet was not mentioned in Domesday Book, but in 1382 it was written as Wyneslee, which was later corrupted to Yiewsley. In the 18th century it was very isolated, lying between the two main coach roads out of London to the west, the Bath Road and the Oxford Road.

The main employment was agriculture at Rabbs Farm and Phillpots Farm and there was also a little local brickmaking. Yiewsley was very rich in brick earth but it was not much used as the cost of transporting heavy loads was then prohibitive. The opening of the Grand Junction Canal through Yiewsley in 1798 made a great difference as far as brickmaking was concerned. There was a big expansion in the brickfields as well as the development of various wharfs and industrial premises along the banks of the canal. Brickmaking was a profitable business now that the bricks could be moved easily by barge. One firm of brickmakers was making at least two million a year. Much of 19th century London was built with bricks made in Yiewsley.

At this time the hamlet was still part of the parish of Hillingdon and it was a long way to walk to St John the Baptist church on Hillingdon Hill for baptisms, weddings and funerals. As a result of the increase of population to nearly 3,000 a chapel of ease was built, St Matthew's, in 1859 designed by Sir Gilbert Scott. In 1874 Yiewsley became a separate ecclesiastical parish, but remained part of the civil parish of Hillingdon until 1896. There were also various Non-Conformist meetings in the area, Baptist, Methodist, Free Church (later called Emmanuel) and Salvation Army.

In 1838 came the opening of the Great Western Railway with its first station out of Paddington in Tavistock Road, Yiewsley. The station was later moved a few hundred yards east to its present position. Yiewsley, with its canal and railway, with branches to Uxbridge and Staines, had a greater potential for industrial expansion than many other centres in the district.

In 1869 a benefactor, Mr Liddell, came to live in Yiewsley from London. He had a house built, the largest in the hamlet, called St Stephen's Villa where much later the Marlborough cinema was situated. Mr Liddell's sons were educated at Padcroft College which was a private boarding school standing in five acres. For that period this was a very superior school teaching Divinity, French, German, Latin, Greek, drawing, mathematics and other branches of a liberal English education. Mr Liddell entered into all aspects of village life and was especially generous to the poor. In the winter there was much poverty because the men in the brickfields could only work in the summer months, and many families who were destitute during the winter were grateful for Mr Liddell's soup kitchens.

In the 1870s a big problem in Yiewsley was drunkenness. Few adults could read or write so the only recreation was in the local inns – and there were many! Again Mr Liddell helped by providing premises to give an alternative place for men to go in their spare time. The Yiewsley Working Men's Club was formed: illustrated magazines and comics were provided, also draughts and dominoes. Tea and coffee could be bought at a low price and, after much argument by the committee, one pint of beer was allowed in a three hour session, to stop the men from drifting back to the public houses.

In 1897 the new Yiewsley Parish Council agreed to erect 17 gas lamps in the High Street, Horton Road and Trout Road. They employed a lamplighter at five shillings a week: as he refused to also clean the lamps this was raised to seven shillings a week.

Few people living in the bustling, traffic ridden district as it is today, can realise what a peaceful hamlet Yiewsley was 200 years ago.

Shepperton Lock

Index

MAIDENSBRIDGE